DNA OF A PASTRY CHEF

Andreas Hein

My Recipes

The recipes in my diary have all been tried and tested. They have either been passed down to me, reinvented, or modernised by myself over the last 50 years and are all listed at the end of this diary. Some of them are more technical and may require a little more baking practice than others. Don't let this put you off trying them out, reinvent them and share your love for baking. My philosophy towards recipes is not to hold on to baking secrets, family recipes, and special creations but instead to share them be proud of them. This way they will always be in circulation, ensuring that the tradition of baking can continue.

Lastly, I beg your pardon. What I am trying to say is be kind to me as this diary was written by me, a non-native speaker, and so it will inevitably have a foreign twang to it.

I would like to dedicate this diary in memory of my grandmother Helene, my mentor, my inspiration, and now my guardian angel.

Contents

Prologue

The European Union, something that I had always taken for granted, was suddenly in danger of disappearing due to a new movement called Brexit. Like so many, I never really thought it would happen. I never dreamed that the foundation that I had created over the last 25 years could disappear like a tray of profiteroles collapsing in front of my eyes. I know not to open the oven door too early when baking a souffle, as it would fall together in an instant, but now I am no longer in charge of the oven. The British people had voted, not realising the impact it would actually have on so many lives, including my own.

I'm not entirely sure if it was my professional or personal journey that brought me to the UK in 1994, but after almost three decades, one can be forgiven for not remembering every detail of one's life. My journey started in the spring of 1970; brought into the world as one of three children to loving parents of German national descent. Now that I am working as a chef lecturer for patisserie and confectionary at a Technology College in Hampshire, UK, I want to take the time to reflect on my professional life as a pastry chef. I would love to share my adventures with you and remember the people who supported, taught, and believed in me. Alongside all of this, I would like to reveal many of the amazing recipes that have been passed on to me, developed, and reinvented by myself over the last 50 years. I will also highlight some historical facts about the bakes mentioned in this diary. Sweet creations have been around forever, so I feel extremely privileged that my life went down that path of sugar and spice and all things nice. My personal baking journey started in 1974, so sit back, relax, and lose yourself in the DNA of sugary treats.

Chapter 1
The early years, growing up and my daily bread

1974-1986

1974, we had just moved into a brand-new house, leaving behind a two-up and two-down cramped makeshift dwelling that provided shelter for the first four years of my life. I left behind a leaky boiler, draughty windows, and my grandparents, who were living next door. Leaving behind the sweet smell of freshly baked goods that my grandmother made every week, a familiar smell, gone!

We moved on the 6th of December, the day Saint Nicklaus popped in for his yearly visit, bringing with him a long list of the good and bad things that my siblings and I had been up to over the last year. He left behind a bag of biscuits that, strangely, looked very similar to the ones my grandmother used to bake.
Maybe she had given Saint Nicklaus her recipes? My favourites in the bag were the cinnamon stars, also known in Germany as "*Zimtsterne.*" Beautifully iced with royal icing and exuding the sweet smell of almonds, sugar, and cinnamon.

Since the 19th century, these beautiful almond biscuits have been integrated as part of the German "Wheinachtsgebäck" selection, but they were first mentioned in 1536. It is believed that the Holy Roman Emperor Charles V was served cinnamon star-shaped biscuits during a visit from Cardinal Lorenzo Campeggio. Spices such as cinnamon, sugar, and almonds were extremely expensive during the 16th century, and they would only have been used in dishes created for the superrich or the rulers of the world."

Over the years, I have tried a variety of Zimtsterne recipes, and although up to 10% of the flour is allowed in the recipe, I have chosen not to use wheat in my version of this delicious treat so that they are suitable for a gluten-free diet as well.

Zimtsterne Page 68

I found it painful not seeing my grandmother every day, and despite only living a 45-minute walk away, for a four-year-old, it seemed that I had moved to the moon. So, I took every opportunity to visit my grandmother, and by doing so, my passion for baking was ignited, and unbeknown to me at the time, it shaped the rest of my life.

Looking back, it might be difficult to understand why I preferred a tiny room in my grandparent's cottage with wonky floors, no toilet or bathroom, and only one running tap with cold water to the beautiful, spacious house with all the mod cons that was my actual home. The truth is that I was mostly attached to the little bakehouse at the side of my grandparents' home, as I found it a magical place to be. To this day, I am still fascinated by how the humble ingredients of flour, butter, eggs, and sugar, together with some skilled techniques, can be transformed into so many delicious pastries ranging from basic bread to the most complex gateau. My grandmother's recipes were all about flavour and time, and she always said that all good things required patience, so her bread making was no different. Her sourdough bread is a simple affair, but with a complex flavour profile. This is achieved by the regular feeding and nurturing of the sourdough starter cultures. The way she used to talk about her sourdough starter, also known as wild yeast, was like she was talking about a family member, not helped by the fact that she called it Helga! To this day, I still name mine and encourage everyone else growing their own to give it a name, as this will provide the love required in your bread-making.

Historically, some believe that sourdough was accidentally discovered in Egypt around 4000-3000BC when someone forgot a piece of dough in the humid conditions along the banks of the Nile. When they returned later, the dough had greatly expanded, so they took the dough and mixed it into a new batch of bread, resulting in well-risen loaves. It was a great change from the flatbreads that were more widely known at the time. Essentially, a sourdough starter is a wild yeast that you can grow from flour and water, in contrast to using commercially produced yeast. By growing your own yeast, the flavour profile is much better, but the disadvantage is that it will take much longer to make bread products. In the 19th century, with the introduction of commercially produced yeast, sourdough production declined rapidly, not helped by the fact that in 1910, a UK government bill was passed preventing night work and restricting working hours. The commercially produced yeast supported the new working conditions, as bread could now be produced much quicker. Hence, sourdough fell out of fashion. Luckily, sourdough started to become more popular again during the 1980s, and nowadays, artisan bakers are going back to basics and embracing the humble sourdough once again.

If you are fortunate enough to know someone who is willing to share their sourdough starter with you, take it and say thank you. If not, here is my version of how to grow your own.

Sourdough Page 69

Things were finally looking up when I started school in 1976. I was not only a very good baker's assistant, but I was able to see my grandmother every day as the new school was only five minutes away from her house. The little bakehouse, however, was only in operation one day per week, so on a Friday night, I stayed over at my grandparents, ready to start baking on Saturday morning. We prepared the dough on Friday evening, ready to rest throughout the night. I know now that by doing so, a more complex flavour profile can be achieved in dough products, but less yeast is also required. One of my favourites was brioche, as it was so rich in eggs, butter, and sugar. A good brioche dough requires a long rest in a cold place before being shaped and baked, as with so much butter, it would be too soft to be moulded.

Brioche started its humble beginnings in Normandy, France, and the name is derived from the French word "broyer," meaning to pound, referring to the long periods of kneading. In the 17th century, brioche became popular in Paris, and here, it was baked in its typical fluted cylindrical shaped tin. A mixture of bread and cake, this beautiful dough made headlines in the 18th century during a riot due to a bread shortage. It was Marie Antoinette's infamous response, "Qu'ils mangent de la brioche," roughly translating into "Let them eat cake," that made brioche available to the masses. This generous gesture was not really that lavish, as the brioche in the 18th century only had small amounts of butter and eggs and, in essence, was not that different from common bread.

Brioche Page 71

4 a.m. Saturday, I could hear my granddad getting up, as his main responsibility was getting the baker's oven fired up, something that would take a couple of hours. I have no idea how my grandmother always knew what temperature the oven was, as her only thermometer was her hand that she waved around in the hot oven chamber. Thankfully, ovens have evolved, so this ritual is no longer required. No heat was ever wasted, from the fierce inferno used for breads and passing to a gentler warmth over the cakes and biscuits to the kissing of the last heat to dry out meringues. Any remaining heat left in the oven was used to warm up the slippers, worn during the evening's rest after a hard day of baking.

A lovely soup rounded up the evening meal along with a beautiful wholemeal and caraway seed bread that we had baked and served with lashings of butter. When she scraped the butter off the knife at the edge of the sliced bread, she called it a pony. I am not sure why, but we always got a pony with bread, and not many children could brag about getting a pony from their grandma!

Wheat flour, the basic ingredient in bread, has been around since 7000 B.C. It was probably first found growing wild as grass mixed with ryegrass. In its endosperm, the heart of the grain, were the right proteins that, when mixed with water and then kneaded, formed the elastic gluten needed for the formation of dough. When baked, the dough becomes bread. The broad category includes both whole grains, such as rice and barley, and milled grains, such as cornmeal and pastry flour. Whole grains are grains that have not been milled. They usually have a shorter shelf life than milled grain. Milled grains are polished to remove the germ and the bran. They have a longer shelf life than whole grains, but some of their nutritional value has been lost. The term granary is believed to be a registered trade name of Rank Hovis Limited and is used to describe their malted wheat grain flour, which contains whole malted wheat pieces that give the bread a characteristic texture. During the early to late 19th century, brown bread was seen as inferior, so only the poor would get it. The upper classes favoured white bread as it was seen as a superior staple. My classic granary seed bread is made with the addition of caraway seeds. Not only does it improve the taste of the bread, but it also aids the digestive process. Caraway seed is related to dill, fennel, and anise, dates to the Stone Age, and has been used for culinary as well as medicinal purposes. In German folklore, however, parents placed a dish of caraway seeds beneath their children's beds to protect them from witches. They believed that objects that contained caraway could not be stolen. Other stories included it being used in love potions, added to feed chickens, and homing pigeons in the hope that the chickens would not wander off and the pigeons would find their way home. During Queen Victoria's reign (1837-1901), the use of caraway seeds grew in popularity due to all things German becoming fashionable.

Granary Caraway Seed Bread Page 71

School was never my favourite place to be, but then again, how could it ever compete with my grandmother and her bakehouse? What I did learn very quickly was that both school and spending time with my grandparents were places of learning. I am a great advocate of learning in a formal as well as an informal setting. Whenever life gets too much, just bake a simple treat and enjoy the pleasure that it can provide. One of the treats that we used to bake was a kind of biscuit or cake known as "Nussecken". A crunchy sweet made with roasted hazelnuts, covered in glossy golden caramel, sitting proud on a bed of buttery, melt-in-the-mouth sweet pastry, cut into triangles and each corner coated with shiny dark chocolate.

Food historians traced the first Nussecken recipe back to around 1700. Created in the German state of Bavaria in its second largest city, Nüremberg, by a baker under the name of Wilhelmus Branntwein. It was during the Polish occupation that, due to a food shortage, this Bavarian baker created a confectionary only made from flour, nuts, and water. The recipe developed further with the addition of sugar and was first recorded in 1763 in Bamberg, a town in Bavaria whose origins date back to the 9th century. With the increased use of chocolate, these nutty triangles were perfected over time. In 1998, the recipe made a comeback due to the Eurovision Song Contest. The German entry singer, Guido Horn, sang about his love for these biscuit bars and started sharing his mother's recipe. After that, everyone was baking Nussecken again.

The recipe I would like to share is also my mother's creation.

Nussecken Page 72

On the 30th of December 1983, my world fell apart when my beloved grandmother and life's mentor died, leaving a massive void within me. I found comfort in the opportunity that was given to me to spend time with her and to say goodbye, although I didn't know then that it was our last time together. The years afterwards were tough. School was more difficult and baking slowly disappeared from my life. Other family members passed away, and with each funeral, I found it harder to understand how to make the best of the life that we were given. Funerals are often followed by a wake, and the baked goods provided on such occasions often have a hidden meaning depending on how well-liked the deceased was. A well-liked and loved person, like my grandmother, had a crumble cake filled with butter and fruits. Omit the fruits, and you were liked but maybe not loved as much, and by providing just the crumble cake without any fillings of butter or fruit, well, you get the idea.

The German custom of the funeral cake, also known as "Zuckerkuchen," translated meaning sugar cake, is, in fact, served at a wake as well as during a wedding celebration. The idea behind this tradition, serving the same cake on both a joyous and a sad occasion, is to highlight the connection between both events and their relationship to each other. I believe that in order to truly experience joy, one has to be exposed to sorrow, and the Zuckerkuchen reminds us of that. The origin of the cake is unclear, but in the mid-19th century, it was prominent in and around Bremen, the second-largest city in northern Germany. This versatile bake, also known as "Freude und Leid Kuchen," translates into joy and sorrow cake and is made by topping a simple sweet dough generously with butter, sugar, and flaked almonds.

My recipe is made with the addition of fruit and crumble. Making any type of yeast dough can be time-consuming, but over the years, I opted for the sponging method in most of my doughs. When using the sponging method, yeast is dissolved in tepid water or milk and combined with some flour. This mixture is then left to ferment before combining with the rest of the ingredients. This will speed up the fermentation process, which is an advantage when making enriched dough. However, it may lack flavour as a slower fermentation produces a better taste.

Zuckerkuchen Page 73

I can't quite remember how I got to the end of my years at school, but I do recall that it went on forever, wasn't enjoyable, and I couldn't wait to be released from the shackles of education. When the day finally arrived, my teacher told us that when we get older and have experienced life, we would all wish to go back to the days at school. I am still waiting for this day, and somehow, I think it was more wishful thinking on his part. In the summer of 2023, I went back to Germany and ended up meeting my friend from my school days. It was the first time that I had seen her since we left school in 1986. It was a lovely experience to meet up and exchange nearly 30 years of our lives in three hours. She also told me that she never felt the desire to go back to school, and we both agreed how wrong our teacher was at the time. Maybe I was not too odd after all!

Chapter 2
Training, military and chocolates

1986-1992

In 1986, school was out, and despite my earlier passion for baking, I could not imagine becoming a baker, as the middle-of-the-night start times were most disagreeable to me as a 16-year-old. I started an apprenticeship as a chef instead, as I would have to make desserts, too. Unfortunately, or looking back at it now, fortunately, a good apprenticeship was a long way away from home, so I left my family and all that was familiar to me to pursue my dream. Strictly speaking, it was half a dream because, deep down, my grandmother kept telling me to follow my heart. Looking back, learning to cook did not provide the initial enthusiasm that learning to bake might have provided. However, by taking this slight diversion, I crossed paths with the most beautiful human being, my now-long-life friend, who has always supported, guided, and believed in me. Our only downfall was that we were both rather partial to ice cream, and this gradually turned into an obsession of daily consumption regardless of the season or time of day.

Ice Cream has a very long list of historical facts, which, quite frankly, would be a book in itself. In essence, it is either made from a frozen custard or a frozen fruit puree, both of which contain accurately calculated amounts of sugar. Too high a concentration of sugar acts as an antifreeze, and you end up with a sweet soup. When I was growing up, I was always told that Italian ice cream was the best, and indeed, I would agree.

With Germany's post-WWII economic boom, the country signed a number of immigration treaties and, in the 1950s, allowed large numbers of Italians to move to Germany in order to counteract Germany's labour shortage. Quite a few of the workers settled and opened ice cream parlours all over the country, while others arrived at the beginning of spring and disappeared again at the end of autumn. It is very similar to bird migration, except the Italians seduce you with their exceptional knowledge and production of ice cream during the warmer months of the year. Some research into ice cream has taken me back as far as 4000 years to China. However, in Europe, it is believed that Alexander the Great (356-323 BC) introduced a form of ice cream as we know it today. With no refrigeration on offer, ice houses were built from 1800 onwards so that the harvested winter ice could be stored, and among other things, the production of ice cream took off.

Vanilla Ice Cream Page 76

There were four of us sharing the top floor of an old guest house, where we each had a room with limited space and cooking facilities. This did not stop us from creating elaborate seven-course dinners, all cooked on two hot plates and a table-top oven. I was the only chef apprentice; my friend trained in all aspects of hotel management, and another was specialising in restaurant management. For the fourth one, we never knew exactly who he was or what he did; he was just part of us and made up the numbers at our posh dinner parties, all complemented by the best two-litre bottle of Lambrusco wine we could afford.

The summer desserts on our menu included a vanilla and grated Sicilian lemon zest semolina pudding enriched with egg yolks and double cream, served with a sharp raspberry coulis. The raspberries were carefully liberated during a night's raid at a local allotment, which made them taste even better.

Semolina, a coarsely ground wheat milled from durum wheat, has a long tradition of being used in German kitchens in their desserts. Mostly eaten at breakfast time or served to babies or those lacking teeth, many older people refused to eat semolina pudding due to its association with WWII and the fact that semolina was often the only food source during the conflict. In the 1980s, however, we saw a revival of basic staple foods made into more gastronomic delights, and despite my best efforts to reinvent my version of this simple dish, my other grandmother refused to even try it.

Semolina Pudding & Raspberry Coulis Page 76,77

One of the most inventive pre-desserts I made was during the winter months in the form of a granita, a kind of scraped sweet ice, flavoured with peppermint liquor and fresh peppermint leaves. The inventive part was making it without a freezer by sitting the mixture of sparkling wine, sugar, and peppermint in a tray on the snow-covered rooftops of our humble abode, genius!

According to legend, Sicily was occupied by the Arabs in the 9th to the 11th centuries, who brought with them a recipe for a drink named sherbet, which was an iced drink made with fruit juice or rose water. During the winter months, snow and ice were taken from Mount Etna, stored in natural caves, and then used to make iced drinks. Ice was simply placed on fruit and flower syrup, but later on, this drink evolved into the Sicilian lemon and almond granita.

Peppermint Granita Page 77

My apprenticeship as a chef was a good one; the hotel was a medium-sized building including two restaurants, a function room, a bar, and a wonderful terrace overlooking the fast-flowing river below. Bavarian cream was a classic dessert during the late 1980s, a rather strange dish comprising a gelatine set of vanilla-flavoured cream combined with schnapps-soaked pumpernickel bread, a type of German rye bread.

This bread, made from coarsely ground rye flour, originates from the Westphalian part of Germany around the cities of Cologne and Düsseldorf. Pumpernickel is made up of pumper and nickel. Many have studied the heritage of this bread, and the result is that nickel comes from Nickolas, meaning victory, but later was changed to "Old Nick," meaning bad spirit or little devil. As for "Pumper," meaning flatulence, you can work out the meaning yourself when you put the two words together. This low-in-gluten bread with an exceptionally long shelf life was given to soldiers and renamed "Schwarzbrot" black bread due to its very dark colour achieved during a 16-20-hour steam bake.

Pumpernickel & Vanilla Cream Page 77

The summer months added extra pressure as many hotels and cafes had the opportunity to open their outdoor spaces. We did have a lot of competition, but on the other hand, the hotel where I trained was the only venue in the town that was fortunate enough to have a large outdoor river terrace and, consequently, was always jam-packed during the summer. In July 2021, I sadly learned that the town of Gemünd, the place of my first apprenticeship, was badly hit by summer storms and flooding. The beautiful hotel terrace overlooking the river had been torn away from the main building. Like so many other buildings, it was unable to withstand the sheer force of nature. Later on, I saw images of the devastation, and it felt like a million years away from the countless apple pies that we had to make in order to satisfy the outdoor diners on that very terrace.

In July 2023, I visited the hotel again, and the scars of the flooding were still visible, even after two years since the river burst its banks. The hotel was still closed and looked sad- an empty shell and a shadow of its former self. Overcome with emotion, I suddenly noticed a sign next to the entrance door, and it read, "Wir sind ein Ausbildungsbetrieb für Gastgewerbe" meaning we train in all aspects of hospitality. It might seem odd, but I felt proud that my professional journey started at this very hotel, and I was suddenly overcome with happier memories.

German Apple Pie Page 78

We also served buckets of "Rote Grütze," a red berry pudding thickened with cornflour and served with silky smooth vanilla sauce.

The origin of this typical summer dish is unclear, as both northern Germany and Denmark claim it to be their invention. In the UK, a similar version is poured in a pudding basin laid out with white bread, which, since the 19th century, has been known as summer pudding.

Rote Grütze & Vanilla Sauce Page 79

Three years later and I had completed a very successful apprenticeship. Despite all the cooking and making some desserts, I had the burning desire not to give up on the baking dream, something my grandmother would have approved of. It was only through working in a hotel that I discovered the possibility of training as a pastry chef without the dreadful early starts that were associated with working in a bakery. Some distant family connections opened the pathway for a pastry apprenticeship in Germany's former capital, Bonn. Situated on the outskirts of the city centre, it was one of the most beautiful pastry shops I had ever seen. I remember my day of the interview as if it were yesterday; window after window was opulently filled with chocolate Easter bunnies, Easter eggs, cakes, and pastries. Inside, the splendour of gorgeous, handcrafted cakes, torten, sweets, and bakery items continued, with the added bonus of the sweet smell of heaven. A huge counter in the centre of the shop was filled with 56 varieties of chocolates, something that was advertised on every bag in the shop; hence, I have never forgotten this magic number of 56 varieties of handcrafted chocolates. I knew then that this was the place I would like to train for the next two years. When I finally started my apprenticeship on the August the 1st 1989, only a few months after my interview, I could not have been more disappointed. All but a few chocolate creations had disappeared from the shop windows and from the huge counter in the centre of the shop. Had I been dreaming about all these chocolates? I always did have a vivid imagination! I soon learned about the nature of the chocolate disappearance, and it had not been a dream or my imagination, nor had it been an exaggeration on my part. It was simply the fact that chocolate is a seasonal product, and therefore, not much of it is about in the height of summer. How clever of all the special events, Christmas, Easter, Valentine's Day and Mother's Day- not to be in the summer! The chocolate Rocher's, however, were available all year round, so this is a good time to share this basic recipe of sugar-roasted flaked almonds combined with carefully tempered dark, milk, or white chocolate.

Almond Rocher Page 79

Tempering is the process by which chocolate is made workable so that the end product has a good gloss, a hard surface, a long shelf life, and a brittle snap when fractured. In order to achieve well-tempered chocolate, melt the chocolate in a water bath and aim for a temperature over 40^0C but not higher than 50^0C. Once melted, pour 2/3 of the melted chocolate onto a cool surface such as a marble or granite worktop, and cool down to around 25^0C by moving the chocolate with a palette knife. Place the cooled-down chocolate back into 1/3 of the remaining warmed chocolate and aim for a temperature of 30^0C-31^0C for dark chocolate, 29^0C-30^0C for milk chocolate and 28^0C-29^0C for white chocolate before being ready to be used. Tempering takes a little practice, but by doing so and with some patience, you will soon get the hang of it.

Chocolate Tempering Page 125

My head pastry chef during my second apprenticeship was a lovely man full of knowledge, patience, and magic, which, fortunately for me, he was willing to share. Here, I learned the secret of the house special gateau, a nut-based cake soaked in rum, topped with a chocolate mousse and ribbons of the egg yolk brandy known as Advocaat, before being smothered in lightly whipped vanilla perfumed cream and covered in hand-shaven glossy white chocolate curls.

Advocaat, a Dutch liqueur made from brandy mixed with egg yolks, lots of sugar and vanilla, nutmeg, or cinnamon, is also linked to the Caribbean and South America, where it was made with avocados instead of egg yolks, hence its name.

As in so many German desserts, Advocaat is the twist in the rather complex structure, and although rather time-consuming to produce, it's worth its weight in gold and, once made, is very special indeed.

House Gateau Page 80

Being so close to the capital city, Bonn, and the pastry shop being one of the finest in the area, we provided sweet pastries and bakery goods to the German government. It never crossed my mind who would be receiving the goods we had made, so in essence, it did not matter to me if Mrs. Schneider from next door bought a cake that I had made or the German Chancellor. However, when Germany was reunited in late 1989, with the fall of the Berlin Wall, I was shocked and horrified that the owners were not happy about the unification of the German people. Instead, they were worried about the government moving to Berlin and consequently losing business.

The communist government of East Germany began to build a barbed wire and concrete wall in 1961, also known as the "Antifascistische Schutzwall," between east and west Berlin. The wall was intended to keep the so-called Western "fascists" from entering East Germany and undermining the socialist state. Eventually, the wall was extended across the east of Germany, and consequently, Germany was divided for nearly 30 years. Not actually realising at the time that I was witnessing history being made, I did feel a sense of joy and freedom when the announcement was made on Thursday, 9th November 1989, that the Berlin Wall had fallen.

Surely, that must be a very important event for Germany and its people, so why could my employer not see that? It was the first time I witnessed how money and greed could overrule a person despite such a joyous event for so many. When I finally qualified in 1991, I decided to move on and learn from kinder and more compassionate people.

1991, being a male and in Germany, I had a slight life diversion due to the compulsory attendance of fifteen-month military service. The whole concept of violence, learning how to use guns, and eating horrible biscuits and dehydrated foods, quite frankly, terrified me. My only option was to apply for a non-military alternative, and despite being three months longer than the National Service, I went for it. I was so stressed over the whole process and the fear of being rejected and then being forced to join the military that it was only my Prince Regent Cake who calmed me down and helped me finally achieve successful approval. I had never been more relieved in my life, but I guess my grandmother was looking out for me; after all, she taught me the recipe, but I had never made it without her.

In 1886, the Prince Regent Cake was established in the royal household of the King of Bavaria. It had eight layers, with each layer representing one of the eight original regions of the kingdom of Bavaria. King Ludwig II was deposed by his minister in 1886, and his uncle Luitpold took over the king's affairs. Three days later, King Ludwig II died and would have been, by rights, succeeded by his younger brother Otto. However, the younger brother Otto of Bavaria, in line to the throne, was equally seen as mentally unstable, so Uncle Luitpold took over his affairs as well. Consequently, he was given the title of Prince Regent, a reign lasting from 1886 – 1911. As the rightful king was still alive, Luitpold was never given the title of king and remained Prince Regent for the entirety of his reign. The cake is said to have been created by the baker Heinrich George Erbshaeser, who, upon introducing the cake to Luitpold, was granted permission by the Prince Regent to christen the cake "Prince Regent Cake."

I remember a version of the cake from my grandmother, a cake made only for special celebrations such as weddings and Holy Communions, but for myself, avoiding the possibility of joining the military, it seemed a good enough reason to be celebrated with royal approval, so this cake was just perfect.

Prince Regent Cake Page 81

You could call it lucky, as I was offered my non-military service in a rehabilitation hospital. Best of all, I was given the opportunity to spend the next eighteen months in the kitchen. Music to my ears, and on my first day of service, I was greeted by the head chef, who was clearly excited to gain a qualified chef and pastry chef without paying top wages. I don't know what came over me, and within a split second, I told him that I had changed my mind and wanted to be trained as a medic during my time at the hospital. He never spoke to me again, and I ended up looking after stroke patients and amputees, one of the most valuable times and experiences of my life.

Hospital food was not the best, but the rice pudding was scrumptious, a recipe I managed to obtain, not exactly the conventional way; well, we leave it at that.

The humble rice pudding is so full of historical facts that are difficult to pin down.

This delicious dessert, or a version of it can be found on every continent. Basically, it consists of rice, milk, and sugar, with the addition of citrus zest and/or spices such as nutmeg or cinnamon. The rice pudding can either be made on the stove or in the oven. Despite it being a little more time-consuming, to make it on the stove, the pudding has a much creamier consistency. This is achieved through the constant stirring of the rice during boiling as the rice grains are knocked into each other and, by doing so, releasing the naturally occurring starch.

Rice Pudding Page 82

I loved my time during the non-military service because I learned numerous life skills, met amazing people, and had a few close shaves. One of which involved me drawing up a very large syringe to clean out a pressure sore on a woman's buttocks. It was a simple medical procedure, but when the woman asked me how long I had been a nurse, I foolishly replied that I was a chef and not a nurse. As soon as I shared this information, my heart stopped beating for a second. The woman looked terrified, but I managed to calm her down with my pastry charm. After that, I always made sure that I got her an extra helping of rice pudding.

Chapter 3
Freedom, abroad and finding my feet

1992-1994

In 1992, Freedom Day arrived. I was finally released from training, college, and army obligations, and after I calmed down, I felt a little lost as to what the next part of my journey would entail. Would I work as a chef, a pastry chef, or leave the profession altogether and become a full-time medic? I finally decided to go back to the beginning, and I accepted a position as a commis chef in a four-star hotel in St. Moritz, Switzerland. After all, it was just for the winter season, so if things didn't work out, it would have only been for a short while. I settled in quickly and met a lot of like-minded people. I was enjoying my freedom away from home in a foreign country, cutting up meat, gutting fish, making stocks, soups, and sauces, learning how to ski, and generally having fun. But it was not meant to be as, once again, my grandmother wheeled her magic over me. I ended up being moved from the main kitchen to the pastry kitchen because the pastry sous chef had broken his leg skiing. As I was a qualified pastry chef, they asked me to cover. After that, I never went back to work in a main kitchen, and my destiny was set to develop my pastry career. Strangely, I don't remember too much about this season except a carrot cake recipe that customers requested for breakfast.

It might seem strange to use a vegetable such as carrots in a cake batter, but as sugar only started to be widely used in Europe from the 16th century onwards, the humble, naturally sweet carrot provided the perfect sweetness to many cakes and desserts. During WWII, the British Ministry of Food promoted that by eating lots of carrots, the ideal eyesight would improve, which would be beneficial for seeing in the dark during the blackouts. This simple "lie" led to many carrot recipes being passed around, and consequently, the carrot cake helped to defeat Germany in WWII as the German Luftwaffe could not locate where to drop the bombs during these backouts. It was also a great sugar alternative once more, as sugar was at the top of the rationing list. Carrots were first grown in the 17th century in the Netherlands and have been used all over the world to sweeten cakes. In Switzerland, however, the carrot cake became popular during the 19th century, and to this day, it is one of the most popular cakes to celebrate a birthday.

Most Swiss carrot cake recipes are made with nuts or almonds; if that is not your thing, just omit the ground almond from my recipe and replace it with plain flour.

Carrot Cake Page 84

Another season followed, now the summer, again in St. Moritz, and this time, I moved up to a five-star hotel and was employed as a commis pastry chef. Here, I was given the opportunity to learn from the best. My head pastry chef, a Dutchman, was kind, knowledgeable, and willing to share, train, and teach all things patisserie and confectionery. The whole experience of working in such a prestigious place felt very Upstairs Downstairs, and each day ended with the silver flatware being counted and locked away for another day. Some of my favourite recipes included the Engadine Nuss Torte, a regional speciality.

In Switzerland, the country is made up of various cantons. St. Moritz is in the canton of Graubünden, and it was here in the region of Engadine that this nut cake was invented in 1926 by the baker Fausto Pult. So far, so good, but the climate in Graubünden is very cold, in fact too cold to grow nut trees, so it seemed strange to me to have a cake containing nuts as their speciality. After some research and many theories being discovered about the origin of nuts in Switzerland, I discovered that many bakers during the Middle Ages moved to Venice and, for over 300 years, specialised in making sweets. When they were expelled in 1766, many came back to the region, so it is believed that a version of the nut cake recipe came from these wandering bakers. In the 1960s, the 'Engadine Nuss Torte' became widely available, and my version of this rather sweet treat I learned in Switzerland in 1992 from my Dutch pastry chef. In essence, it is a lidded shortcrust pastry tart filled with caramelised walnuts and honey.

Engadine Nut Cake Page 85

It was a short season of only three months, ending abruptly with a knee operation followed by a full-leg plaster cast while still in Switzerland. Unfortunately, I had been driving from Germany to Switzerland in my car and was now stuck on the mountain, in a foreign country, with a car and leg in plaster. Once I broke this news to my parents, they made their way to Switzerland on a rescue mission by train with the aim of picking me up and driving us all home. St. Moritz is a relatively small place, and it was virtually impossible to find accommodation for two nights during the high season so that my parents could have a rest before that long drive home. After some research, no mobile phone or Google, I managed to find shelter a bit further up the mountain in a convent, a slight detail I left out when I told my parents that I had found them a room for two nights. It was a, simple affair, but a good breakfast was provided by the nuns. In fact, according to my parents, they provided the best Bircher Muesli they had ever eaten. My mum, not one to hold back, managed to obtain this recipe from the Mother Superior, and we all use this simple but delicious recipe to this day.

Bircher Muesli, a very popular breakfast around the world, has been credited to its creator, Dr. Maximilian Oskar Bircher Benner, who created his version in 1900. A medical professional with strong beliefs that healthy nutrition was not only the cure for many ailments but that a healthy diet would be the key to preventing people from getting ill in the first place. After a hike in the Swiss mountains, he was served a mixture of oats and milk, very similar to the Bircher Muesli. With a few adjustments, he brought it to his patients as a healthy start to the day.

Mother Superior Bircher Muesli Page 86

During my knee recovery at my parents' house in Germany, I managed to spend some quality time with my mum, and this time she was in charge when it came to baking. Most Sunday afternoons were set aside to bake waffles. I first made these with my grandmother in 1975, when she told me a little secret. She told me that she was the oldest of nine children, and it was down to her to bake the waffles on a Sunday. As there were so many to bake waffles for, and the best waffles were eaten warm, she never managed to get a waffle herself because, by the time she finished baking, all had been consumed. The problem with waffles is that once you start baking the first one, the smell of this freshly baked treat travels for miles. On many occasions, it is not surprising to find a neighbour or a stranger in the house who was just passing by, as the smell was too strong to resist. Back to the secret: once you have baked your first waffle, eat it, as this way, you will have at least managed to get one. If you are, however, caught eating the first waffle, just convince the waffle-eating catcher that this needs to be done for quality control purposes. I have never forgotten this secret, and still, to this day, I eat the first waffle despite the fact there are always plenty of them to go around.

Historically, waffles have a long history; some included pilgrims sailing from Holland to America in 1620, taking the Dutch waffle with them on their voyage. In 1735, the word waffle appeared in print, and when Thomas Jefferson returned to the U.S. from France in 1789, he brought with him not only many French waffle recipes but also the long-handled waffle iron to make the waffles. By the time he became the third President of the United States in 1801, the popularity of the waffle had spread throughout America. Waffles were further enriched with molasses, sugar, and maple syrup, as well as being served with chicken and kidney stew. The Dutch-American Cornelius Swarthout of Troy received a patent for the first waffle maker in the USA in 1869, or to be precise, on the 24th of August, which to this day marks National Waffle Day. The famous Belgium waffles have been made since 1964 and are traditionally made with a light yeast batter and served only with a dusting of icing sugar.

Waffles Page 86

My knee was recovering nicely, and due to a lack of mobility and my mum's constant baking, my waistline started to expand, but how could I refuse all her baking without offending her. I knew, and she knew, she was my feeder, and all I can say to that is thank God we had tracksuit bottoms with elasticated waistbands. On a more positive note, I used my time sitting around to research many of the recipes mentioned in this diary. It did become very clear very quickly that food is definitely one of the best ways to bring different people and cultures together and break down perceptions and barriers. My mum was serving up another of her bakes, this time her famous "Bienenstich Kuchen," the bee sting cake. When I asked her how this cake came about, she simply replied that she had learned how to bake it from her mother, my other grandmother, who was refusing to try the semolina pudding that I had made.

It was the bee sting cake that spurred me on, not only to eat her cakes, but it wouldn't be so bad if I knew a little bit more about them. Luckily, my sister proved to be very helpful in providing books and baking magazines from the local library to support my research. Google was not even a word back then, and sometimes - and only sometimes - I wish we didn't have the internet today.

My research for the bee sting cake took me back to 15th-century Germany. The sweet cake, topped with caramelised sliced almonds and filled with custard, vanilla buttercream, or whipped cream, was created by German bakers and confectioners who lived in the German town of Andernach. According to legend, this all happened in 1474, when the inhabitants of the neighbouring town, "Linz am Rhein," attacked the residents of Andernach. The conflict was created by the German Emperor, who took access to the river Rhine away from Linz and granted it to those living in Andernach. The attack was successfully defended by the people of Andernach when they started to throw whole hives of bees at the attackers. Victory was celebrated with the creation of the bee sting cake, and many versions of this cake have been created since.

In my own memory, we often had this cake during the summer months when sitting in the garden, and here, the sugar and almond-coated cake always attracted bees. Many got stung by bees while trying to indulge in this cake, and I always thought that it was the battle between bees and humans that this was the reason why the cake got its name. When you think about it, it is not a million miles away from the original tale. The bee sting cake is a complex affair to get right as it is a combination of two contrasting items, such as a sweet dough covered in caramelised almonds, which needs to be protected from humidity, and a light custard filling, which needs to be kept cool. Due to a lack of refrigeration, this cream-filled cake only really took off in the 20th century, when fridges became readily available.

Bienenstich Page 87

Now, fully recovered, eating lots of mum's cakes and mountains of recipe research, I was given the opportunity to spend three weeks in July on Föhr, Germany's second largest island in the Frisian island group in the North Sea. I was working in a fish restaurant making desserts, and here I learned about the national dish Futjes, a kind of cream cheese doughnut made without yeast, deep fried in sizzling hot oil before being coated in cinnamon sugar- so delicious, and so satisfying to bake and eat.

I discovered that these little doughnuts were made in the 16th century from sourdough and semolina, which was later replaced with ground almonds. This then-traditional Christmas treat was developed further at the beginning of the 20th century, and with the growing popularity of baking powder, the recipes were reinvented and used to celebrate the New Year.

For myself, I associated the Futjes with the region that I grew up in, where we call them "Mutzen," a traditional deep-fried bun to celebrate the regional carnival season, which starts on the 11th of November and finishes six weeks before Easter.

Futjes Page 88

After my short stay on the island, I travelled to Denmark, spending some time with my lifelong friend and her sister, sharing a log cabin by the sea. It was a time to reflect, recover, and work out the next part of my professional journey. Despite being in a self-catering establishment, my friend and I were keen to try some Danish recipes, some more, some less successful, but still better than anything my friend's sister could come up with. Her speciality was only burned toast. Burned is a nasty word, so to be kind, we called it caramelised breakfast. She, my friend's sister, did ask me once how I remembered this, and to her misfortune, we do have photographic evidence. It is not all based on Legoland in Denmark. In fact, at this time in my diary, I would like to share my Danish pastry recipe.

I am often asked what the difference is between the dough for a Danish pastry and the dough for a croissant. Well, the croissants should talk to you once baked, making that lovely crunchy noise when torn apart. On the other hand, the Danish pastry is soft and quiet. The noise difference is simply achieved by using water in the croissant dough and milk in the Danish pastry.

Back to my recipe for Danish pastries, the origin of this delicacy, according to a Danish chef I met in Switzerland, was that in the 1840s, Master Baker Albaek of Copenhagen, Baker to the Royal Court, began to make Danish, which was puff pastry based on yeast dough. "Vienna" pastry was brought to Denmark by Austrian bakers who were hired to replace Danish bakers during a strike. The Austrians left behind their methods of rolling butter between the layers and then letting it rest before shaping and baking. Danish bakers, who left the country to travel, brought their knowledge with them, and it has become a favourite all over the world. Hence, the Danish pastry, as we know it today, was born.

Before embarking on this scrumptious recipe, I would like to share a little tip with you. As these pastries are rather time-consuming to make, I suggest that you double or triple the recipe. Once you have made lots, put them in the freezer once assembled, but before they have had their final proof or baked. Take them from the freezer as required, tray them up, defrost them overnight in the fridge, and bake them the next morning. Finish once baked.

Danish Pastry Page 89

After the beautiful summer of 1993, I found myself again at a crossroads, not knowing what to do. After a little research, I found a vacancy as a pastry chef in a family-run but one-star Michelin restaurant in the Black Forest, a mountainous region in the southwest of Germany. Here, I was in charge of the pastry section, which was terrifying and exciting at the same time. The owners were kind but strict, and the chef patron himself could get very vocal, so I was pleased to benefit from the thick wall between the main kitchen and the pastry kitchen, something my ears equally appreciated. Our signature dish was a goat's cheese soufflé, often served instead of a cheese course. The goat cheese that we used was a locally sourced goat cheese curd, so creamy and subtle in flavour, complimented with the traditional fruit of the Black Forest, cherries that, after being caramelised, were coated in balsamic vinegar, looking like little jewels on a plate.

Goat Cheese Soufflé Page 91

Working on my own and in charge of the pastry kitchen was a good place to find my feet. I had the freedom to push the boundaries of plated desserts and learn to work with locally sourced products. The most closely grown product grew about ten metres from my workbench in the form of a gigantic walnut tree. Harvesting was hard, and it needed everyone on board to pick, drying, crack and process the nuts in all sorts of ways. Here, I came up with a Christmas dessert of caramelised walnut ice-parfait, a posh mousse enriched with sun-golden egg yolks and thick glossy honey, before being frozen (in the freezer) and served with a rich velvet chocolate sauce.

There are some arguments about the origin of walnuts, but a lot of them were found in central Asia, where they can be found wild as well as semi-cultivated. Many believe that walnuts were part of the diet of early tribes of hunter-gatherers, as walnuts provide healthy fats, fibre, vitamins, and minerals.

In my recipe, however, the walnuts are coated in sugar and made into a brittle, perhaps not as healthy, but utterly delicious. An iced parfait is a type of ice cream that can be made without an ice cream maker, so in essence, it is a frozen mousse. The chocolate sauce can be based on milk or water. The milk-based chocolate sauces tend to set when cold, which is due to the milk fat, and, in most cases, this sauce is served warm. On the other hand, water-based chocolate sauce stays runny when cooled down and, most of the time, is served cold, poured over desserts, ice creams, and my walnut honey iced parfait.

Walnut Iced Parfait Page 92

My time in the Black Forest was a great learning experience but tough, and after working 14-15-hour days, I questioned my future once again. I did, however, have some time off as the restaurant was closed two days of the week, always Sunday and Monday, and as they say, do as the Romans do; I started this weekly ritual of driving to Baden Baden, a spa town in the Black Forest. Not only did I enjoy relaxing at the spa, but afterward, the indulgence continued with a creamy chocolate sponge perfumed with Kirschwasser and melt-in-the-mouth dark chocolate shavings, also known as Black Forest Gateau.

Historically, many have claimed to have invented this cream-filled cake. Always perfumed with sour cherries and distilled schnapps. One of these claimants was the pastry chef Josef Keller, who presented the gateau as we know it today in 1915 at the café Agner, which was located in the suburbs of Germany's former capital, Bonn, a mere 500 kilometres away from the Black Forest. The Black Forest Gateau made another appearance in 1934, this time in Berlin, where it gained popularity not only in pastry shops and hotels but also made its way to Austria and Switzerland. Apparently, in 1949, Black Forest Gateau became number 13 in the ranking for best-known German cakes.

For myself, I believe the tales that the cherries on top of the gateau represent the national Black Forest headdress worn by the women, still to this day, and that the hat, also known as "Bollenhut," with its distinct red pom-poms, is a direct link to this delicious cake. My version of Black Forest Gateau is made up of a chocolate sponge, not a cake.

People ask about the difference between a cake and a sponge, and here is my explanation. A cake is usually made by beating sugar and butter, slowly adding eggs before flour, and folding some sort of raising agent. The sponge, however, is created by whisking the eggs and sugar until light and fluffy before folding in the flour and sometimes melted butter, with no additional raising agent being used here other than air created by whisking. This process makes the sponge much lighter and an ideal partner to create a gateau, which, in essence, is a multi-layered confection of sponge and cream.

Black Forest Gateau Page 93

In a strange way, having the same gateau every week for weeks and months on end helped me realise that there are two choices in life. The first is being happy eating Black Forest Gateau every week, and the second is, don't. I saw the Black Forest Gateau representing my professional life as a pastry chef, and even if I changed jobs or countries, I would still be eating Black Forest Gateau. I wanted more from life than being stuck in a kitchen while life was passing me by; surely there must be more to my life than baking? Eventually, I concluded that the hospitality industry was not for me anymore, so I signed up at Karlsruhe University to study tourism as a mature student. The only slight issue with this was when I found out, after I signed up, that 50% of the course would be taught in English, a language not familiar to me other than a few broken words from my school days. Joining an English evening class was one option, but I decided a far better one would be to work in the UK for 6 months, learn the basics, return, and start a new chapter in my life. After signing up with an agency in Germany that specialised in hospitality jobs in the UK, I managed to get an interview within the first week, and best of all, the person interviewing me in the UK spoke German. So far, so good, but I tried to keep the interview a secret from my employer, so my only option was to conduct the entire interview from the only phone box in the village, and to my amazement, the agency connected me to the UK, and the head chef, as promised, spoke very good German. At the end of the interview, he offered me a job at a hotel in a small town called Marlow, a position as a pastry sous chef. Within a month, I packed my life into two suitcases, and on the September 2nd 1994, I boarded a flight to London Heathrow.

Looking back now, with travel and security checks having been tightened to the point of being ridiculous when boarding a plane, it is hard to imagine that my hand luggage included my chef knife box full of knives, cutters, scissors, and piping nozzles. My onward journey took place by bus, but due to my very limited English language skills, I ended up missing the correct stop to get off and found myself on the outskirts of Marlow. God knows how I managed to find Marlow, this beautiful town in Buckinghamshire with this charming-looking hotel situated on the banks of the river Thames, yes, the river I remembered from my English book at school. Finally, I had arrived in the UK.

Chapter 4
Rule Britannia

1994-2002

I entered the Compleat Angler Hotel in Marlow through the front door, shattered from the journey, excited by a new adventure, and terrified at the same time for not understanding any language other than German. My initial fears disappeared quickly when I met the head chef, who greeted me in German. After an hour of chatting, I complimented him on his very good German language skills, which ended in an embarrassing situation when he revealed that he, in fact, was German himself. In my defence, he had been in the UK for over 30 years, had a British accent, and, to me, looked British. Our informal chat ended with a tour of the kitchen and pastry kitchen and an introduction to other team members. The walkabout ended with the announcement that from tomorrow, I would be in charge of the pastry kitchen, including four staff, as the current pastry chef was about to finish her very last shift at the hotel. I had never been so mortified in my life. How could I run a pastry kitchen in a foreign country with people I could not communicate with? Quite frankly, it was a nightmare. Somehow, I managed it with daily English lessons during my break in the afternoon, sign language, and lots of face pulling-not my face! I found my feet very quickly, and apart from bringing my own expertise and recipes to the hotel, I learned for the first time how to make scones.

Despite many stories about the origin of the scones, most believe that they started life in Scotland around 1505. Known as a quick bread that was made with oats before being baked on a hot griddle. Some believe the word "Scone" is associated with the Stone of Destiny, which was used during the coronation of Scottish kings. The medieval kingdom of Dalriada was situated at the northwestern Scottish and north Irish borders and was ruled by the 36th King of Dalriada, Kenneth I. When he first united Scots from the west and the tribe of the Picts from the east of Scotland, he moved his capital from the town of Scone in western Scotland to the Scone Palace, which is situated in Perthshire in the south. Here, the Scone was given its first initial name. Other stories will tell you that the Dutch word "schoonbrood," meaning beautiful bread, was adapted to make the word scone. Despite the rich history of 1505, the humble scone gained much more momentum almost two hundred years later. During the early 1800s, Anna Duchess of Bedford requested her tea be served later in the afternoon with a selection of sweetbreads, and the scone was one of these treats. She loved her afternoon treats so much that they soon spread among the upper classes. In fact, to this day, the scone is an integral part of afternoon tea, where jam and clotted cream complement this simple bread.

Nowadays, scones can be found in all sorts of flavour combinations, from plain, cheese, dried fruit, apples, spices, and lavender-the list is endless! My original recipe from my days at the Compleat Angler Hotel in Marlow has also evolved, and I would like to share my version of the humble scone with you.

Scones Page 96

On my days off, I ventured into London, and I soon realised that if I wanted to make the most of my six months in the UK, I needed to spend some of my remaining time working there. Just after Christmas 1994, I handed in my notice and moved to London to spend my last two months in the capital that offered so many opportunities. I was very fortunate that I had met some very kind people during my visits to London, so I ended up staying at a friend's flat in the north of the city. I worked for a catering agency late afternoons and evenings while, during daytime hours, I learned English at the Camden School of English, where I gained my first official language qualification. I avoided all things German, food, and people alike, so I was forced to only communicate, read

English, and generally adopt a new culture. I managed to visit many department stores, bakeries, and patisseries from right across the world, as well as art galleries, museums, theatres, pubs, and clubs. After all, I was in a city that never sleeps, and neither did I. Time flew by, and when the day of my departure arrived, I decided the best way to say goodbye to my very good friends was by leaving them a parting gift of my Devil's food cake.

This rich, sumptuous chocolate cake has its own annual celebration day on the 19th of May, where it is enjoyed by lovers of chocolate. Some believe that the name of this full- flavour chocolate cake was linked to "Angel Food Cake" as they were in direct opposition to each other, such as in colour, texture, and mouthfeel. The Devil's Food Cake recipe was created in the United States, and some recipes can be found in print as early as 1902. As with so many recipes, it has evolved over the years, so you might find that some of the older recipes use melted chocolate in the cake batter, whereas more modern versions may include cocoa powder. Baking soda is used in this recipe, and when the soda is combined with the melted chocolate or cocoa powder, it reacts chemically, giving the cake its dark reddish colour. Once the baked Devil's Food Cake is filled with dark chocolate icing, it is complete. If you fill the cake with white icing, it becomes the well-known red velvet cake.

Baking soda, or bicarbonate of soda as it is known chemically, is a type of salt that, when combined with liquid, acts as a raising agent. In my version of this cake, I not only like to use baking soda as it helps the cake rise more outwards but also baking powder as this raising agent pushes the cake batter in a more upward direction. When both are combined, it creates a wonderful, light, airy cake mix. Baking soda is one of the most widely produced chemical compounds as it is not only used in the kitchen but also has a firm place in cleaning products and for medicinal purposes. The National Bicarbonate of Soda Day in Germany is celebrated every year on the 30th of December. This is a date close to my heart, as it is the anniversary of my late grandmother's death. I celebrated this day with my Devil's Food Cake, as, like this cake, my grandmother was devilishly good.

Devil's Food Cake Page 97

The cake for my friends in London was baked and decorated, and my bags were packed for my return to Germany. On my way to Heathrow Airport, I was suddenly overcome with a whole mix of emotions, mostly sadness and uncertainty if going back to Germany would be the right thing to do. My heart wanted to stay, but my head wanted to take on the opportunity to start my university course in Karlsruhe. Torn between good and evil, like having to decide between an Angel or Devil's Food Cake, so much pressure, so much to decide, so much-too much!

Then, a combination of circumstances resulted in me missing the plane, and I was convinced that my beloved grandmother was looking out for me. I am forever grateful for the divine intervention, which I believe was the foundation of my new life. Now, in a foreign country with little money, nowhere to call my own but happy, for the first time-truly happy. My very good London friends were slightly shocked, when four hours later, I turned up on their doorstep again. As I wasn't sure what had just happened, the only thing I could think of was that I had realised that I made my parting gift of the Devil's Food Cake too big, and it would have been better if I had helped them eat it. It is quite funny now that my whole life was based on helping my friends eat a cake, and once the last crumb was consumed, I called my parents, broke the news that I would stay a little longer, and after nearly 30 years, I am still in the UK.

My English language skills were improving with every passing day, and I finally ended up in a five-star hotel making afternoon tea pastries. Here, I introduced the Austrian chocolate cake 'Sachertorte', which can be easily recognised by the shiny chocolate glaze and distinctive writing of the word "Sacher" on the top. This version of the rich, slightly dense chocolate cake is sandwiched together with apricot jam. Sachertorte is claimed to be the second-best-known cake in Austria, only just pipped to the post by the famous apple strudel.

Traditionally served with thick double cream, legend has it that the Sachertorte was created in 1832 by a young pastry apprentice by the name of Franz Sacher. At only age 16, he was working at the Austrian court of Prince Klemens von Metternich in Vienna, where he was asked to come up with something new for the prince and his guests to enjoy. The opportunity for this young, aspiring pastry chef only came about as the court's head pastry chef was unwell. With his love for chocolate, the young Franz created the Sachertorte, which became an instant hit with the prince and his guests. With very little time to prepare and pressure from the prince telling Franz, "Dass er mir aber keine Schand' macht Heute Abend!" ("let there be no shame tonight"). Terrified by the prince's comment, the young Franz created the cake with his love of chocolate in mind, and luckily this worked in his favour. In 1876, Eduard Sacher, the son of the then-acclaimed pastry chef Franz Sacher, opened the Hotel Sacher in Vienna. It is believed that the original recipe that Franz created in 1832 is a well-kept secret at the hotel to this day, making this special chocolate cake the hotel's trademark.

I was told once that you haven't been to Vienna if you haven't been to the Hotel Sacher and tried the authentic Sachertorte. Well, I have been and tried it, and all I can say is make your own mind up if you agree that it is, in fact, the best one out there.

Sacher Torte Page 98

I was only working part-time so that I could continue with my studies. After a year of working hard and saving, I wanted to settle into a more permanent living situation instead of sleeping on the sofa at my friend's house. I was going to buy a flat, but in order to obtain a mortgage, I needed to be in full-time employment. Once I approached my head chef at the hotel, he was delighted and offered me a full-time position, but not so delighted with my terms and conditions. However, I did get the job Monday to Friday, 7.00–15.00, unheard of for a full-time pastry chef in a 5-star hotel, but I guess they saw the value in me-and the rest is history. I had heard that a celebrity chef had opened his restaurant in another part of the hotel, and his kitchen was on the same level as the pastry kitchen. I have never been drawn to any celebrity status. I just left it at that. One afternoon, a chef, unknown to me, entered the pastry kitchen with no hat, apron, and long curly hair everywhere, and he decided to take a piece of cake from a tray that I had prepared for room service. Not amused, I told the chef not to touch the cakes that were plated up, and a very angry response came in the form of, 'Do you know who I am'? I did not know who he was other than a rude individual nicking my cake. He stormed off, and I found out later that it was the celebrity chef who had opened the restaurant, and his name was Marco Pierre White. Afterwards, he visited the pastry kitchen many times but now displayed better manners, asking for a piece of fruit cake, and in fact, I grew to like him and enjoyed our little chats in the afternoon.

When I first met the celebrity chef, my thought was, what a fruitcake, but I guess that is a different thing altogether.

I discovered that in ancient Rome, from its founding in 625BC to its fall in 476AD, a mixture of barley, honey, wine, nuts, raisins and pomegranate seeds was made into a type of fruit cake known as Satura. It was primarily made for the soldiers to boost their energy. During the period between the fall of the Roman Empire in 476AD and the beginning of the Renaissance period in the 14th century, dried fruit and spices became more widely available, and Western European chefs started to put fruit in their breads. It was the beginning of some famous European fruit cakes, such as the 13th century Italian 'Panforte' meaning strong bread, and the German fruit bread named 'Stollen', which was created in Dresden, East Germany, in the 1400s. When sugar started to arrive from the Caribbean in the 16th century, fruitcake was developed in more of what we associate with fruit cake today. The new-found gold, called sugar, provided the opportunity to turn fruit into candied fruit and sweeten all sorts of goodies. Sugar became essential as a preservation method, a very useful way to prolong the shelf life of all kinds of foods.

By the 18th century, the fruitcake was further developed with the addition of butter. This now sinful cake was even banned in some parts of Europe for being too indulgent. On February 10th, 1840s, the indulgent fruitcake gained popularity once again when it was served at the wedding reception of Queen Victoria, who had married the German Prince Albert of Saxe-Coburg-Gotha. Some believe it is one of the greatest love matches in British history. Queen Victoria and Prince Albert's wedding cake was topped with a spun sugar figure of Britannia. Traditionally, wedding guests would put a piece of the wedding fruit cake under their pillows, with the hope that their future marriage partner would be revealed to them during the night's dream.

A nice thought, but I can see this getting a little messy, placing a piece of fruitcake under your pillow, so most couples opt for favour boxes now. The top tier of the fruit cake is often reserved for the first-year wedding anniversary, or if the stork is busy during the first year of marriage, it makes an ideal christening cake. Fruitcake is a traditional afternoon tea offering, and although a favourite during the Christmas period, it is made throughout the year. If you, like me, find yourself pushed for time and haven't soaked your fruits beforehand, then try my version of this wicked delight.

Fruit Cake Page 99

Christmas, like everywhere, is a busy time in the hospitality industry, and we started our preparation in August with the traditional soaking of the dried fruits for the Christmas pudding. We produced such large quantities of this festive traditional pudding that no bowl, machine, or mixer was big enough to make it. We ended up pushing all the kitchen tables to the side, lining the floor with plastic sheeting, and mixing and kneading the whole batch, on the floor, at once, attacking this gigantic mixture from all sides using all eight of us pastry chefs. Once mixed, we had enough mix to make 2000 individual puddings.

Also known in America as plum pudding or in Charles Dickens "A Christmas Carol" as figgy pudding, the traditional Christmas pudding is sometimes described as a cross between a haggis and fruit cake that is set on fire. The theory behind this description is linked to medieval sausages made from fat, fruit, and spices that were combined with meats, various grains, and vegetables, before being stuffed into animal stomachs and then boiled. In the early 15th century, a savoury concoction of meat, root vegetables and dried fruit became known as "Plum Pottage," plum being a generic term for dried fruits. Fruits became more widely available by the end of the 16th century, and the savoury pudding changed to a sweeter version. The animal stomach was gradually removed and replaced with a pudding cloth, and another animal product was therefore removed from the dish. Not entirely animal-free, the fat in Christmas pudding is suet, which sits around the kidneys of either cattle or mutton, which not only provides flavour but also contributes to the keeping qualities. By the mid-1600s, this now sweet plum pudding was strongly linked with and enjoyed during the festive period. It was banned when Oliver Cromwell came to power in 1647, as he tried to eradicate all links to paganism and Roman Catholic worship. Along with the then-loved Christmas pudding, carol singing, Nativity scenes, and Yule logs were all prohibited. Fortunately, or at least fortunately for the Christmas pudding, in the 1660s, the English monarchy was restored, and some Catholic customs were reintroduced. When German-born ruler George I came to the throne in 1714, he requested some plum pudding at his first English Christmas banquet, which gave him the unofficial title of "Pudding King."

When I finally returned to Germany in 1998 for the first time in four years, I had planned my visit to my family over the Christmas period. What better gift than to take a traditional Christmas pudding that I had made. Apart from seeing me, they were all curious to find out why I had brought a fruitcake with me. After carefully explaining the difference between a fruitcake and a Christmas pudding, they finally understood that the fruitcake was baked and made with butter, while the Christmas pudding was steamed and made with suet. My mother, a practicing Roman Catholic herself, was the first to try it. She was impressed that the pudding was made of 13 ingredients to symbolise Jesus and his twelve apostles. Once the pudding mixture is made, it should be stirred from east to west to honour the journey of the three wise kings. Lastly, a coin was placed in the pudding before being steamed. My sister found the coin while eating her portion, and when she asked me the meaning behind it, I told a little lie, saying that the person who found the coin had to do the washing up. In actual fact, it represents good luck for the New Year unless you accidentally choke on it or break a tooth. Setting the pudding on fire with brandy represents Christ's passion. My version of the Christmas pudding has more than 13 ingredients in it, so don't tell my mother!

Christmas Pudding Page 100

Another exciting Christmas delicacy was the construction of a giant gingerbread house. It was so big that it was constructed from wood, set up in the restaurant at midnight, and then cladded in over 2000 gingerbread tiles, plastered together with numerous batches of royal icing, and decorated with sacks of sweet treats. By the morning, a beautiful, majestic-looking gingerbread structure had appeared literally overnight. Unfortunately, it only lasted three weeks as it was trashed by two princesses, who were visiting the hotel for afternoon tea. Everyone was too afraid to stop the late Queen's granddaughters, and thankfully for them, I was not working in front of the house.

Like every good gingerbread recipe, it should start with the obvious: the ginger.

My research revealed that a root first cultivated in China was predominately used for medicinal concoctions. Eventually, ginger started its journey as with so many other spices via the Silk Route, and some research has revealed that in ancient Greece and Egypt, ginger was often used during ceremonial events. The first gingerbread recipes appeared in Europe during the 11th century, when Crusaders brought ginger back from the Middle East, and cooks for the rulers of the world started to experiment with it. Early recipes for gingerbread included ground almonds, stale bread, rosewater, sweet vegetables, and, of course, ginger. The mixture was then pressed into carved wooden moulds, removed, and left with an imprint that not only represented current kings and queens but also religious symbols. These early gingerbreads were like newspapers telling stories. If you were wealthy enough, edible gold paint and icing were used to embellish these works of edible art. As spices and sugar became more widely available during the 16th century, stale bread was replaced with flour. In addition, sugar, cinnamon, and cloves were added, together with eggs, making the gingerbread more palatable.

Queen Elizabeth I, had gingerbread made in her own likeness, which she regularly used to impress her guests. Gingerbread also became very popular at fairgrounds, where, tied with a ribbon, you could buy it for the one you loved. As cooling foods was a challenge in most kitchens at the time, broken-up gingerbread was scattered amongst decaying meats to mask the smell. Gingerbread can now be found all over the world, but in Nüremberg, Germany, it is considered an art form. To this day, the gingerbread baking guild is awarded, a tradition dating back to the Middle Ages. In France, Hungary, Poland, and many other countries, including America, gingerbread dominates the festive period.

Going back to the giant gingerbread house that we were creating during the night shift, gingerbread structures such as houses took hold from the 16th century onwards. However, they gained mass popularity after the publication of the fairy tale Hänsel and Gretel in 1812 by the Brothers Grimm. During the same period, German farmers did not have sufficient land available to make a living, which led to mass immigration to the USA from 1816 onwards. As a result, the tradition of the gingerbread house started to take root in America.

Gingerbread Page 101

My full-time employment at the hotel helped me obtain a mortgage, and I managed to find a lovely flat in south London. I decided to move on from making afternoon tea pastries at the 5-star hotel, and I ended up in the raunchier part of London called Soho. Here, I took over the pastry kitchen in an independent chain restaurant where dessert sales were virtually non-existent. The pastry kitchen was basically a table under the stairs with an oven. Over the years, I learned that, in order to succeed, make changes gradually and slowly, and after four years of working at the restaurant, I had taken over 20% of the whole kitchen. A fully established pastry kitchen suddenly appeared and now employed three full-time pastry chefs. At the restaurant, I experimented with making bread, and here I developed my focaccia bread, which I make with mashed potatoes.

Often associated with Italy, this flatbread, topped with olive oil, herbs, and salt, has been given the name focaccia from the Latin "focus" or "heart." The heart refers to the heart of the fire pit, where bread is often baked on the hot stones in earthenware dishes. Bakers are used to puncturing the breads to stop them from bubbling up during baking. The characteristic dimples in the focaccia bread allow the oil that is brushed on top to penetrate evenly into the dough. If you want to be offensive, you could call it pizza dough, and although it is 2000 years older than pizza, they do have some similarities. However, focaccia bread is proofed for longer before baking, whereas pizza dough has a shorter resting and baking time.

Despite strict rules about the height and size of focaccia bread, I am extremely happy with my addition of the mashed potato, which makes it really fluffy, keeps it moist, and is simply irresistible.

Focaccia Bread Page 102

I loved working at the Mediterranean restaurant, mostly because of the people and the freedom to create new dishes. It is unusual to make bread in a restaurant setting, and something I had no great experience with. After my success with the focaccia bread, I carried on creating bread and ended up with a lovely white dough recipe made from a simple bread dough combined with choux pastry. The addition of the choux pastry makes this bread ideal for toasting in dishes such as bruschetta, as the choux pastry used in the dough keeps the bread nice and moist once it has been toasted or grilled.

White Bread Page 103

The success that I had created at the restaurant was soon recognised by the chain. With the support of the head office, I set up training classes on the days the restaurant was closed, as well as a pastry helpline for staff to call if they needed support with their pastry items. Once again, I managed to create my own terms and conditions and went from working 5 days a week, Monday to Friday, 7.00-17.00, to working 4 days and gaining a pay raise. I loved my time in Soho, but after 4 years and meeting so many amazing people and cultures, it had to come to an end, and I decided to move on, but not without my classic crème Catalan and the lemon tart recipes.

Apparently, the "Crème Catalan" is classified as one of Europe's oldest sweet dishes, first made in the 14th century in the north-eastern part of Spain, with some links to the Jewish community that used to live in Catalonia. In Spain, this dish is traditionally made on the 19th of March to celebrate the saint "Sant Josep," who is also linked to the celebration of Father's Day. The crème catalan first appeared in a recipe book from the 14th century and is made from milk, egg yolks, and sugar flavoured with orange, lemon, and cinnamon, creating a much lighter and less firm texture. On the other hand, crème bruleé appeared in French recipe books a lot later, and in the 1691 edition, uses cream, whole eggs, sugar, and vanilla before being set and caramelised with sugar on top. Unfortunately for Spain, the cream bruleé is more widely known, and despite being Europe's oldest dessert, it is lagging behind its French cousin.

In my recipe, I combined the Spanish and French versions and found a happy medium that was extremely popular.

Cremè Catalan Page 103

My next recipe, like so many others, is firmly French, the famous "Tart au Citron," lemon tart or lemon pie.

To make a good lemon, anything, you require lemons, which some believe were originally cultivated in northern India in a place called Assam. However, this hybrid between bitter and sour oranges was not known as lemons at the time but was regarded by early Romans as "Median Apples" after a north-western region in modern-day Iran. Later, when they started their journey via the Silk Route into the Middle East, North Africa, and gradually across the Mediterranean, they eventually became known by their Persian name, "Limu," or some believe from the Arabic word "Laymun." England saw its first lemons arrive from Spain when they were gifted in 1289 to Queen Eleanor of Castille, the first wife of Edward I. In 1493, Christopher Columbus introduced lemon seed to the New World, and by 1565, lemon trees were grown in South Carolina, United States.

The lemon tart, a sweet pastry case filled with lemon custard, can be traced as far back as the 12th century, and Quakers made a version of it in the 18th century in America. One of the first known lemon pie recipes was discovered in a cookbook written by an American, Philadelphia-based cook under the name of Mrs. Goodwell. She not only ran a pastry shop but also organised cookery lessons, a woman after my own heart. Allegedly, one day, she had too many leftover egg whites and turned them into meringue, which she spooned over the lemon pie before baking. However, other researchers have found that the lemon meringue pie was invented by Swiss pastry chef Alexander Frehse in the 1800s. In France, the tart au citron became popular in the 19th century in the wake of the French Revolution, but my recipe appeared on the dessert menu in Soho Soho, Frith Street, London, for the first time in September 1997.

Lemon Tart Page 104

In May 2001, my pastry journey took me back to a 5-star hotel, this time the Churchill Intercontinental, located just off Oxford Street in London. Here, I was in charge of a large pastry section, making and creating lots of items for various restaurants at the hotel, room service, afternoon tea, and banqueting. Amongst the many desserts that we made, I remember making lots of chocolate truffle torts, a recipe I still use to this day in my wedding cakes.

Originally the recipe was derived from the chocolate truffle itself, a mixture of cream of chocolate and boiled cream, known as ganach, cooled down before being rolled into balls and coated in cocoa powder. Many claim the invention of chocolate ganache, but one of my favourite stories concerns an apprentice to the famous chef August Escoffier in the 1920s. The young apprentice had accidentally poured hot cream intended for a bowl of beaten eggs and sugar into a bowl filled with chunks of chocolate. Once the mixture had cooled down, it began to harden up and was rolled into truffles.

My truffle torte is a mixture of chocolate and cream, but the cream is whipped rather than boiled before being set on a gluten-free chocolate sponge base and dusted with cocoa powder.

Chocolate Truffle Torte Page 105

I did enjoy working at the hotel, but something was missing, and I had no idea what it was, so out of the blue, I decided to leave the hotel only after a few months of being there. My timing in handing in my notice could not have been worse. On September 10th, 2001, I submitted my resignation to the food and beverage manager, and despite being offered a pay raise, I was set to leave in four weeks' time. The next day, the atmosphere changed when most of the staff were crowding into the staffroom, glued to the television. Here I was witnessing the terrible unfolding of 9/11, and with this tragic event, hospitality came to its knees, and very quickly, you could see the disappearance of pastry chefs all across the world. I did manage to hang on until Christmas, but I was now in charge of opening boxes of pre-made desserts as most pastry staff were dismissed due to the lack of guests staying. I was finally replaced with a chef de partie doing my job at half my salary.

Despite the dark month that affected the industry, there was a little light on the horizon for the Churchill Hotel. The onsite restaurant under the name 'Clementines' was due to be taken over by Italian chef Giorgio Locatelli and turned into his independent Italian restaurant. The restaurant was due to open in the spring of 2002, but in late autumn 2001, he hosted a dinner to celebrate his new adventure, and I was trusted to make his famous "Tiramisu" for the evening banquet. I remember Giorgio as an extremely passionate chef full of enthusiasm and kindness, so it was my honour to make his version of this Italian classic.

"Pick me up," the translation of this well-known Italian dessert, started to appear on dessert menus around the 1960s, in the way we might know this classic recipe today. However, historical records reveal that this coffee-flavoured delight was invented in Treviso, an Italian province not far from Venice, in around 1800 by a "Signorina," who ran a brothel in Treviso. She created this aphrodisiac sweet dish for her customers in order to restore her client's energy levels before returning home to their wives. In other words, she supplies her clients with a natural Viagra. Full of nourishing and rejuvenating ingredients such as sugar, eggs, mascarpone cheese, sweet biscuits, and not to forget coffee and cocoa. Alcohol was added much later, and it is widely debated which best to use, from marsala wine amaretto to rum.

I have made many versions of this recipe, and the one I made for Giorgio Locatelli can be found on many websites. One of my personal adaptations is the "Tiramisu" gateau, a recipe I would like to share here.

Tiramisu Torte Page 106

I took some time off and once again found myself at a crossroads. The industry was changing. I was getting tired of working long hours, a lack of social life, and the stress it caused in personal relationships. In February 2002, I did find a new job as a head pastry chef at the prestigious Sheraton Park Lane. A large section with lots of responsibilities and pressures awaited me. As it was still very difficult to find a decently paid head pastry chef job, I took on this new role despite my better judgment. I remember one banqueting dessert in particular, which was the soufflé - yes, the humble soufflé created on a mammoth scale for up to 700 guests. Made, baked, and served with military precision, quite frankly, impressive!

Soufflé, literally translated into "to blow up," is a sweet dish often linked to the famous French chef Vincent de la Chappelle, who created many culinary delights for many European dignitaries, including the mistress of Louis XV, Madame de Pompadour. A detailed account of how to make the perfect soufflé was published in 1814 in the cookery book "The Art of the Cook." The recipe was provided by the French chef Antoine Beauvilliers, who himself is credited with the first grand hotel in Paris. The soufflé has had many adaptations over the years, but the main ones are the hot soufflé, which is a custard base with folded meringue, and the pudding soufflé which is a little more stable as it is a roux, or flour-based with folded whipped-up sugary egg whites. Regardless of the type of baked soufflé, according to French chef August Escoffier, "Kings wait for soufflés; soufflés do not wait for kings." In other words, despite following the best soufflé rules in the world, soufflés only have a very limited lifetime if you want to enjoy the ultimate soufflé-eating experience.

Cinnamon Pudding Soufflé Page 107

Due to its larger function room capacity, the hotel ballroom was very popular with Jewish bridal parties. A separate kosha kitchen was used, and all kinds of dishes were made under the watchful eyes of a rabi. Apart from the strict rules of using separate kitchen equipment and utensils, I also learned that meat and dairy should not be eaten together. Three to six-hours breaks ought to be observed in between the two. During a wedding function, guests would expect meat, so that inevitably resulted in all desserts having to be made dairy-free. I love learning about different cultures and foods, so I found it an interesting time to learn about Jewish customs. One of the petit fours we used to make regularly was the "Lekach," a type of honey cake not that dissimilar to German ginger cake or Yorkshire parkin. Many recipes have been adapted over the years, some made with water, tea, or, like the Jewish community in Austria, coffee. However, they all contain honey, as in the Jewish New Year, it is seen as a symbol of sweetness to come.

Lekach Page 108

One of my lasting memories from my time at Sheraton Park Lane is of a function that brought together all the great chefs of that time. This prestigious event required months of planning and organising. It was, of course, an honour to be part of it, so we decided to showcase some of our pastry skills with over 40 sugar pergolas. Constructed out of pastillage, an icing sugar and cornflour paste set with gelatine. When soft, the icing is pliable. When dried out, it becomes like porcelain and can be glued together with royal icing.

It's been around since the 17th century and became popular during the 18th century as many wealthy homeowners used to show off their dinner tables with sugar sculptures made from pastillage.

As pastillage has been admired by so many over the centuries but was in sharp decline, what better way to present our homemade chocolates and petit fours than on these impressive sugar pergolas? They were skillfully handcrafted over several months and presented to the industry's high and mighty on the night of their celebration.

I remember that at the end of the meal, all the kitchen and front-of-house staff were called into the ballroom and applauded and congratulated by these industry experts. We were so proud, and months of planning and preparation had indeed gone down very well. At the end of the meal, the beautiful sugar structures were left on the tables as a further part of the table decoration, but they became anything but. In 2002, smoking was still allowed in restaurants across the UK. As the evening advanced and the alcoholic beverage gained momentum, our beautiful pastillage pergolas were turned into ashtrays by our so-called honourable guests. When they finally returned to the kitchen, many had been broken, and most of them were contaminated with nicotine and cigarette butts. Thanks a bunch, my fellow chefs. Don't get discouraged by this story, and if you fancy having a go at pastillage, try out my recipe, but you need your own imagination to create something magical.

Pastillage Page 108

The little life I had was truly over; very early starts, very late finishes, and endless functions were starting to take their toll on my mental health, something I could not ignore. One evening, the executive chef walked past me; in his words, he said, "Andreas, you have a face like a slapped arse; what's up"? I guess what he was trying to say was, "My dear Andreas, why does your face look so dissatisfied? My response, not planned or intended, was that he should start looking for a new head pastry chef. What I wanted to say was that I hated being here; I did not like the working culture, and apart from being exhausted, I felt frustrated with the workload that was expected of me. Unlike the head chef, I was less direct on this occasion. I left in August only after a few months, slightly worried about the future but at the same time feeling the weight of the world lift from my shoulders.

Chapter 5
Education and trips aboard

2002- 2004

The summer of 2002 started once again with unemployment, a loss of direction, and yet another crossroads. Why was it that the baking profession could provide so much pleasure but, at the same time can be such a hard and stony road?

I considered myself a good pastry chef, but my passion for the profession was fading; my heartbeat for baking was slowing down. What if my grandmother had been wrong all along, and this was not meant to be my path in life? All the doubts and conflicts that I had developed were suddenly rescued by the spiritual awareness that I had created, some manmade and learned, some naturally occurring as I got older. I always strongly believed that life is a train journey with many stops, allowing people to get on and off. Every part of that journey is an opportunity, a time for learning, reflecting, and growing into the person we become. In my view, life is all about choices, so why choose just one direction? Maybe it was time to go down another path. I kind of knew all that, but I could hear my grandmother's voice saying, "Don't lose the dream and look at all the different ways to achieve your dream." Deep down, I knew there was another way to rekindle my passion for baking: to make my pastry heart beat again and let the light shine bright once more. The answer is to get into teaching.

A magazine, really, yes, the Hotel and Caterer magazine offered me the opportunity to come across a position as a pastry chef lecturer at a college in Farnborough. I was living in south London at the time, and Farnborough did not seem a million miles away, but I soon discovered that I had been looking at Farnborough in Kent, whereas the job was in Hampshire, a million miles away. I wasn't very confident about getting the job anyway, as, after all, I was only a pastry chef with no teaching experience. As a backup plan, I applied for another job with Tesco as a pastry development chef. In the early years of the millennium, supermarkets started to offer freshly made desserts, which provided the opportunity for many experienced chefs like me to explore different routes. The job was in York, but the interview was in Birmingham, and as such, I had to create a few desserts. Once made, I carefully packed them into a cool box before boarding the train to Birmingham on one of the hottest days of the year. When I arrived, I was given 30 minutes to set up my dessert before presenting my ideas, followed by the interview itself. One of the desserts that I made was a champagne raspberry jelly sitting elegantly on a rosewater panna cotta in a disposable plastic champagne flute.

The dish of sweet milk, cream, sugar, and gelatine is often associated with Italy, but panna cotta, meaning cooked cream, is a relatively new invention in terms of its name. During the 1960s, chef Ettore Songia offered the milk jelly-like dessert under its current name in his restaurant, and although some associate it with the northern Italian region of Piedmont, a version of this dish has been found in a cookery book dating back to 1879, where it was known as "latte inglese," English milk. The French blanc manger or the Danish moos hwit are very similar but maybe less well-known. Like Panna Cotta, the jelly topping in my recipe is also set with gelatine. This setting agent was first used in ancient Chinese and Egyptian medicine more than eight thousand years ago. Derived from animal bone parts, it is an important ingredient in cookery as its setting ability lends itself to stabilising foods and controlling their texture.

Champagne Jelly & Rosewater Panna Cotta Page 110

I was not sure if it was my jelly, any of the other desserts, my experiences as a pastry chef, or if they liked me as a person, but they offered me the job. I was pleased, so could this be another route to reignite my passion for patisserie?

As I was still contemplating not only starting a new career as a pastry development chef but also moving to York, a letter arrived stamped Farnborough College of Technology. Ever the optimist, I thought it was kind of them to let me know that I was unsuccessful with my application. To my amazement, they had invited me for an interview as a pastry chef lecturer. The letter stated that I was required to give a presentation on sugar boiling and asked if I needed an overhead projector or PC for a PowerPoint presentation. I had absolutely no idea what either of them was or how to use them, so I opted for good old-fashioned note cards.

Caramel can be tricky business to get right, but to make it easy, I differentiate between wet and dry caramel. Dry caramel is made by simply heating a pan and slowly adding sugar, which will melt into the golden lava we know. You do need to be careful, as it can burn quickly. Water or other liquids can be added, and once again, I offer caution as the caramel is close to 150^0C, and your added liquid is nowhere near that temperature, so stand right back and have a pan big enough to avoid scalding yourself. Wet caramel is made by boiling sugar with water until most of the water has evaporated, turning the sugar into golden caramel. Whichever way you choose to make caramel, it is essential to use clean equipment and clean sugar, avoid stirring during the boiling process, and wash the sides down of the boiling sugar with cold water and a brush. If you get foam building during the boiling of sugar, remove it with a spoon. Lastly, have a bowl of cold water to hand and place the pan into it once the required colour or temperature has been achieved. This will ensure that your caramel will not turn black, which is also known as sugar couleur.

Caramel Page 110-111

Some believe that the Arabs discovered caramel around 1000 AD. In America, hard caramel, also known as hard candies, was made in 1650, and over the century, various experiments led to a variety of textures being created by adding fats such as butter, cream, or milk. Despite caramel being many years old, salted caramel, one of the most popular flavours to date, only gained popularity in 1977 when the French pastry chef Henri Le Roux added salted butter to his caramel. The Brittany-based confectioner took his creation to the 1980 Paris Salon International Patisserie Fair, where his salted butter caramels were declared the best confectionary that France had to offer. The craze for salt in sweet dishes continued, and in the late 1990s, Pierre Hermé introduced his salted butter caramel macaron. By the millennium, salt was used in the production of chocolates, ice creams, and even vodka fell victim to salt!

During my interview, I was extremely nervous, and I got my note cards all mixed up. After analysing the interview panel for about 30 seconds, I decided that none of them would know anything about sugar boiling, so with no other options available, I blagged it. I was wearing my first ever suit, and unfortunately, a week prior to receiving the interview letter, I had a haircut, which I hated and, therefore, decided to shave all my hair off. I must have looked like I was on remand or had nits, but either way, I got the job and started on the 5th of September 2002.

I was greeted by my new colleagues with a bath towel draped over an office chair, a kind of custom that Germans have when going on holiday. The thinking behind this ritual is that by getting up really early, placing a beach towel on the lounger before returning back to bed with the expectation that they, in fact, had reserved the best seat on the waterfront. Unfortunately, I did not get the joke with the towel, so I made my first impression on the workforce: typical German, no sense of humour!

The beginning of a new academic year always starts with an induction period where the first-year students arrive all excited with an abundance of new chef uniforms and waiters' kits. Of course, how silly to assume that they would have checked their uniforms before bringing them to college. After all, their parents only spent about £300 on their new attire, so needless to say, half of it did not fit, or items were missing, which became clear during a fashion parade on the first day. It's funny, but from the first few minutes, I knew who was going to be trouble, who was eager to show off their culinary knowledge, and who had never heard of a napkin. The aim of the course was to train young people in the kitchen as well as in front of the house, which can be difficult if some have only been inspired by making fairy cakes at school.

Year two and three students returned a week later with surprise and curiosity to find a new lecturer in residence. They didn't take long to accept me, and only a week later, I was asked by one of them how she could get her hands on the morning-after pill. I can't remember if I blushed at this point, and I did not realise that questions like these would be as common as being asked how to make caramel.

I have always enjoyed passing on knowledge, and with my passion for patisserie, I started my teaching career with lots of enthusiasm. I had to come up with a plan of what to teach, and with that, I was introduced to my first scheme of work. It sets out what skills have to be taught, including the aims and objectives for each lesson. I consider myself quite organised, so this way of working suits me fine. I liked the structure, and it helped me prepare the lessons. Lesson one, Chelsea Buns and Devonshire Splits, was taught to a group of eighteen school leavers trying to navigate through a new start at college, some excited, some less so, but all present and correct.

The Chelsea bun is made from a sweet yeast dough enriched with butter, sugar, and eggs, and as these ingredients are heavy for the yeast in the dough to lift, it requires almost twice as much yeast as in the same amount of flour in a bread dough. Furthermore, the enriching ingredients brown very quickly, so the oven temperature should be lower than when baking bread. On the plus side, the butter, sugar and eggs add additional moisture to the dough, which will slow down the staling process, so you can keep them a little longer than bread products.

The Chelsea Bun is a derivative of the cinnamon roll and was first produced around 1700 at the Chelsea Bun House in Chelsea, in one of London's more affluent areas.

These buns were not only firm favourites of the Royal Family, poets, and artists but soon gained mass appeal. When afternoon tea became a popular affair during the 18th century, many regions created their own versions of sweet buns, and the ones in Devon were named Devonshire splits, also known by some as "Chudleighs Bun." Like scones, these sweet buns are split in half and filled with jam and cream.

Chelsea Buns & Devonshire Splits Page 112

During the initial demonstration, with students asking questions and me trying to engage all learners, it all seemed calm and organised. Then, sending them off to their workbenches, replicating the shown task was like a scene from the Lion King where the wilder beasts run off in all different directions with the lion, alias me, trying not to get run over. However, I soon got the hang of it, and after a few lessons, I was in control like a conductor navigating an orchestra. I soon became aware that learners do play different instruments, some needing more or less help during their performance.

I was finding my feet, but a few weeks later, I was faced with another challenge after a fairly quiet pastry class. I ended up being left in the kitchen alone with a female student and a support worker when I realised that the girl had a little accident in the form of having wet herself. I tried not to make a big thing of it and asked the support worker to sort her out, and as far as I was concerned, the matter was dealt with. To our surprise, we later learned that, in fact, her waters had broken, but despite this, I was spared the task of midwife that evening. I heard about the expression a bun in an oven, but now I know that there is more than one oven.

I never realised that sex education would be part of the job that a lecturer teaching cookery had to do, but I am now regularly confronted with teaching the subject of birds and bees during weekly tutorial sessions. I am not exactly an expert, but I soon learned that school teachers aren't either. We are always trying to link non-hospitality subjects into the field of catering, and over the years, we have become rather good at this. For example, a banana is the perfect object to demonstrate how to put on a condom, and you would be amazed at what you could do with jelly.

Banana Cake Page 113
(No bananas have been ridiculed or used for any other purposes than to make banana cake.)

I mentioned tutorials a few times by now, and if you are not familiar with the term, it is a weekly lesson where the whole year group comes together. Random subjects that are set by the college are being taught, from health-related issues to current affairs. It is also an opportunity for students to interact with others from different courses during cross-college events. We also use this time to track a learner's progress and provide time for a one-to-one chat. During individual tutorials, I am often confronted with personal issues, and apart from the professional progress of a student, their welfare is equally important. Having to teach a whole raft of subjects you are not familiar with is something I learned over the years because nobody actually tells you these things when you apply to teach cookery. On one occasion, a student complained to me about another member of staff, which sometimes happens and must be addressed. The complaint involved a student, another member of staff, and a leek. It sounds a bit like a joke, but not at all a laughing matter, as the other member of staff allegedly hit the student with the leek, and I don't think it was to tenderise it. I questioned the member of staff about the incident, and to my surprise, it did actually happen. The member of staff was, in fact, my boss, and he responded with, well, he deserved it!

The incident with the leek reminded me of the potato and leek pasties that we regularly make to sell in our onsite college pastry shop. Pasties are often associated with Cornwall, the most southwestern county of the British Isles.

During the 13th century, only the best ingredients of venison, beef, lamb, seafood, and fruits were encased in shortcrust pastry and indulged in by the upper classes and royalty alike. One of the reasons it was a popular dish for the wealthy was that the kitchens were often a long way away from the dining spaces, and by encasing these precious foods into pastry, they stayed hot for a much longer period of time. This concept of keeping food warm by baking it in pastry was soon adopted by Cornish farmers and miners from the 17th century on. The food in the pasties was not only kept warm, but they used to carry their pasty lunch under their clothing, and with that, it provided extra thermal insulation as well. The pastry had to be stable so it could be dropped down the mine shafts, and some even placed a savoury filling into two-thirds of the pasties, whereas the other third was stuffed with fruit, so both a main and a dessert were provided. Another important factor to consider when making these pasties is the strong, thick edge known as crimping, which nowadays provides a decorative appeal. In the mines, however, they provided the perfect handle to hold the pasties and, therefore, not only keep the food clean from dirty hands but, most importantly, to avoid arsenic poisoning, which could otherwise have been transferred from hand to mouth.

Potato Pasties Page 113

Violence is never a good disciplinary tool, and students must be protected at all costs with lots of care and attention, but unfortunately, this can't be said for the lecturer. Once, we were asked to take on a student. I know it seems odd to take students onto a hospitality course, but on this occasion, we had little information on the learner, and to my surprise, we took him on regardless. It worked out OK for the student, but only for a while before he threw in the towel, and only then did we learn that, in fact, he had been in prison for attacking a teacher. After that experience, I had to think back to the incident with the leek, which suddenly seemed trivial.

As you might have guessed by now, English is not my first language, which, in the grand scheme of things, is not important but has provided me with some amusing confusion. When making a quiche, we tend to seal the shortcrust case after blind baking to avoid a soggy bottom and let's face it, nobody likes a soggy bottom, not even the girl whose water broke during my lesson. Back to the point, I told the students to seal the tart case with egg wash all over, and most of them got it, but there is always one, and, in his case, he egg-washed the inside and then took the case out of the ring, turned it over, and sealed the outside because I did say all over.

The word "quiche" is derived from the German word "Kuchen," or, in English, cake. This dish is often linked to the medieval European region known as Lothringia, which is now known as Germany, Belgium, and Luxembourg. Eggs and creams became popular in Italy during the 13th century and, as early as the 14th century, gained momentum in many English dishes. This well-known savoury pie with an open top was a skillful dish to master as it requires delicate and gentle heat to avoid the eggs and cream splitting, something open fires did not provide. If you had to name a type of quiche, you would probably think of Quiche Lorraine, and I often wondered if the person who first made it was named Lorraine? Some research, however, has revealed that this tart, filled with smoked pork lardons, Gruyere cheese, onions, and nutmeg, has its origins in the north-eastern region of France called Alsace and Lorraine. Originally, this region was part of the Holy Roman Empire, where most people spoke German. Charles III, the Duke of Lorraine, became Duke after his father's death in 1545 at only age two, so it was his mother, Christa of Denmark, who became Regent until he reached maturity. After Lorraine was invaded by France in 1552, Lorraine became part of northeast France, but the young Duke was taken and raised by the French royal court as it was of great advantage to the French. When he finally took over the reins as the official Duke of Lorraine, he started to write about the former region of Lothringia and the famous quiche Lorraine.

The popularity for quiche gained momentum again in 2023 when it was requested by King Charles III to be one of the official coronation dishes.

Savoury Flan (Quiche Lorraine) Page 114

I had been teaching for a few years now, and with the help of my teaching qualifications, I became more confident and eventually realised that I should have studied childcare. To me, it seemed that lecturing is more about childcare than teaching a professional skill. Having slowly adjusted to this fact, I was then confronted with the biggest challenge yet. A group of 14-year-olds from school on a school link programme, which was a nicer way of saying disruptive behaviour, is another thing they don't tell you during an interview. Well, I was hit like a tsunami by a bunch of learning-impaired individuals who, apart from smoking and having phobias against safety shoes, had little interest in food unless it involved ketchup. After a number of months in battle, but with careful military precision, I eventually managed to turn a corner and transform these extremely testing teenagers into fairly decent home cooks. They could even make a light and springy Victoria sandwich filled with strawberry jam and Chantilly cream, apart from the odd one, but then again, you can't save them all.

As you might imagine, the Victoria sponge cake is often linked to Queen Victoria, who enjoyed a slice of cake with her afternoon tea. But firstly, let me clarify the confusing word combination of "sponge, cake." In my view, it does not exist as it is either a sponge or a cake. Keep up as I have already explained the difference earlier on when I was making my Black Forest Gateau. So, the official wording is Victoria sandwich, which consists of two cakes filled with jam and whipped or buttercream. Cakes and sponges were in production well before Queen Victoria took the reins. In fact, a version of the Victoria sandwich was recorded in the Spanish Renaissance period in the 15th century and in 17th century England. However, the texture of the cakes was more like biscuits or bread, as yeast was used to leaven the cakes. The Victoria sandwich really came into its own with the invention of baking powder by Alfred Bird in 1843. Alfred's wife, Elisabeth Bird, was allergic to yeast and looked to her chemist husband for answers to replace yeast in bread with an alternative. Eventually, after many trials, he came up with a formula of tartaric acid, sodium bicarbonate, and corn-starch, which together formed the first complete baking powder. Not only used in some breads, but the baking powder also took cake-making to a whole new level, including the perfection of the Victoria sandwich. Apart from the many bakers who loved his invention, his wife was eternally grateful, and due to her allergy to eggs, he came up with custard powder, first and foremost, to please his wife. The trend of using baking powder continued across the world, and in 1859, US chemist Eben Horsford further developed self-rising flour by using monocalcium phosphate. He then went on and combined the successful bread-raising agent with soda bicarbonate and blended both with corn-starch, and this concoction became "Rumford Baking Powder." Germany was not far behind in the new raising agent trend with their version of this magic product, introduced in 1893. Pharmacist Dr. Oetker, a household name to date when it comes to baking, introduced baking powder to the domestic market.

The filling of the Victoria sandwich has been hotly debated, and the cake itself has fallen victim to scrutiny in many competitions, from the Women's Institute to the Great British Bake Off, including the best type of jam or whether whipped cream is better than buttercream. My recipe is simple, and the jam really doesn't matter. It's all about personal preferences. Do I add vanilla or citrus zest? Who cares? But please remember this: do not call it a 'Victoria Sponge Cake'.

Victoria Sandwich Page 114

Being a lecturer is extremely hard work, but on occasions, it can be fun, never more so than when on a college outing. My first excursion was to Brussels on a bus with a bunch of second years on their end-of-year trip. After some confusion with the bus driver, we finally arrived at the hotel, and it only took about three hours for the excitement, from a lecturer's point of view, to diminish by the minute. Having left the hotel for about an hour to find a suitable restaurant for our students to dine in on the first night, we returned only to be greeted by a slightly tense hotel manager. He irritably informed us that some of our students had to be taken off the hotel's roof, and with that, we also discovered that most of the darlings were nine sheets to the wind.

On that night, I learned from a more experienced lecturer how to patrol students' bedrooms last thing at night or, in fact, all night. Despite wanting to respect their privacy, it does pay off that during room inspections, one must not forget the wardrobe, as it can house more than coat hangers. During our first round, we did find some boxer shorts in the girl's wardrobe. It was not unusual, but on this occasion, they were still on one of the boy, and it was the only item of clothing he was wearing that evening. The rest of the night was OK, apart from the room where one of the boys, in a state of intoxication, smashed up the hotel's bedroom furniture. I was glad that I was in possession of a skillset that allowed me to repair broken wooden furniture. Eventually, I managed to fix them all with a large tube of superglue purchased from the local 24-hour corner shop. Now, the glue is always part of my luggage, regardless of the trip.

We do try to make trips educational, and on the trip to Brussels, we included a visit to a cheese factory and beer breweries. One of the best excursions was to a fish farm, where we were shown by a very enthusiastic owner how they smoked the fish. A very detailed demonstration of how the smoke was produced ended up with most of the students having to leave the smokehouse due to their inability to inhale the smoke, only to be found outside smoking a cigarette. You can't help but love them. The trip also led us to a small artisan chocolate maker, and I found it most inspiring that these beautiful truffles could be made on such small premises, something I could see myself doing from home one day. It always fascinated me how some of the best chocolates were made with Belgian chocolate. How and where was chocolate grown in Europe? A lot of chocolate is being processed in Belgium, hence the title Belgian chocolate, but I did find it sad that there was little or no information available about where the cocoa beans were grown. Consequently, there wasn't any recognition of the countries or the growers that did all of the hard work, something I set out to change later on in my career.

B ack to the Belgians and their strong association with chocolate, which some say goes back to 1635 during the Spanish occupation of the country. Cocoa was making its way to Europe from Central America, and by the 18th century, it became a favourite drink amongst the rich and wealthy. By the late 19th century, chocolate had become more accessible and affordable to the masses as cocoa beans were being imported from African colonies. Despite Europe's strong association with Africa's cocoa imports, this did not lay the foundation for the Belgian chocolate industry until much later. Belgium's export market for its imported cocoa raw material, in other words, the famous Belgian truffles, only really gained momentum in the 1960s, and by the 1980s, it had grown into a worldwide household name.

These might include familiar brands such as "Côte d' Or," which started to make chocolate bars in 1911, or Godiva chocolates, available since 1926. A new invention of "pralines," or filled chocolates, gained popularity at the end of the 19th century and the beginning of the 20th century, but as to the Belgian truffle, there is some debate as to its origin. The word truffle comes from the Latin for "tuber," meaning "lump." The shape of the chocolate truffle is representative of the fungus-shaped truffle found on forest floors, and the coating of cocoa powder mimics the dirt of the woodland soil. The mixture of cream and chocolate, that once set, rolled and dusted in cocoa has records linked to 1850 at the Paris patisserie and confectionary shop "Siravdin." Others claimed it to be a Swiss invention, but I like the tale I mentioned earlier when, in the 1920s, an apprentice of the famous Auguste Escoffier accidentally poured hot cream over chunks of chocolate instead of the egg and sugar mixture it was intended for. Not to waste, these expensive ingredients were rolled into balls, and once the ganache had set, the truffles were finished with cocoa powder.

You will find many recipes nowadays that include alcohol or long-life cream being used. In my opinion, the best chocolate truffles are made with fresh double cream and good quality, sustainably sourced chocolate. By doing so, you can create a beautiful truffle, but with the disadvantage of a short shelf life of only three days. Use of long-life cream and alcohol increases lifespan to 2-3 weeks.

Truffles Page 115

I was getting used to college life; every day was a school day with new challenges, both professional and personal. I was working towards my certificate in teaching and education, mostly evening classes, which was tough, especially after a hard day of teaching and before a one-and-a-half-hour journey back to London. The alarm, at 5 a.m. the next morning, triggered the whole day again. However, I really enjoyed the new job, but I also enjoyed living at my flat in south London. I regularly met up with a friend who was living close to me, taking it in turns to host a dinner at either mine or her place. We often talk about it now, and one of the things she always brings up is the choux pastry swans that I used to bring back from college, something I barely remember, but what are friends for?

The choux pastry swans we used to make at the college are, as the name says, made from choux pastry. This twice-cooked hollow delight can be used in both sweet and savoury dishes. The choux, meaning cabbage, was given its name as the baked choux buns looked like little cabbages. The firstly boiled and then baked or deep-fried pastry was created in France by an Italian chef by the name of Pantanelli, who served under Catherine de Medici of Florence. Not only was she a woman of great Italian aristocracy, but she went on and became Queen of France in 1547 when she married King Henry II. Pantanelli followed her from Italy to France, where he created the choux pastry known as "Pâte à Pantanelli. Over the years, like so many of these recipes, they were improved and perfected. During the early 19th century, the pastry chef Antoine Caréme created what we know as profiteroles while working at the French court of Marie Antionette.

The hollow interior and crisp out layer are achieved by water being used in the recipe that, during baking, turns into steam, pushing the pastry up and making the flour and egg set. If that process of baking is interrupted by opening the oven door too early, your choux products will collapse. We follow a golden rule in the pastry kitchen: if you see choux buns in an oven that do not belong to you, do not touch or open the oven door.

Many sweet and savoury treats are made from choux pastry and include the famous profiterole that, when stacked high with caramel, serves as the French wedding cake known as "croquembouche." Other familiar items are long finger-shaped eclairs, meaning flash in French, as they can be eaten in a flash, whereas in Germany, they are known as love bones, "Liebes Knochen."

An annual French cycling event starting in 1891 took place between Paris and the city of Brest, and to eventually commemorate the event, pastry chef Louis Durand of Maisons-Laffitte, a small town outside Paris, created the iconic choux pastry ring in 1910. At the original race organiser Pierre Giffard's request, the choux rings symbolised a bicycle wheel and, when cut in half, were filled with hazelnut cream and fresh raspberries, although other fillings were being used.

In recent years, the choux pastry trend has been given a facelift with the introduction of craquelin, a biscuit-like paste rolled out thinly and placed on the piped choux pastry before baking. During the baking, the biscuit layer will crack, creating a crunchy top, and by colouring the paste, a different look is created altogether. I have included how to make craquelin as part of my choux pastry recipe, as well as hazelnut-flavoured custard.

Choux Pastry Page 116

Time flew by in the new teaching job, so it was almost time for another college trip; experience has taught us that over the years, it is good to vary the trips. One of our favourites is going to Paris, well most of the time to Disneyland. It's a great trip, as you don't actually see the students all day and spend the time going on the rides yourself, eating ice cream and apple doughnuts. It sounds great, but believe me, the evenings and nights are challenging. One year, we were located on the ground floor, which provided the perfect opportunity for the students to room hop via the windows instead of using the squeaking hotel room doors. We were left with no other choice than to exit the room through the windows ourselves, which was more challenging for some, and positioned ourselves outside on the lawn to observe any nocturnal activities involving British catering students. At this point in my career, I had accumulated lots of experiences with students away on trips and could foresee most things. Therefore, I adapted my night-time patrolling strategies accordingly. But as they say, you never stop learning, and, on that evening, we were walking past the rooms on the outside of the hotel, when we came across an open window belonging to a group of our students of non-British origin. I also noticed a cooking smell, and to my amazement, I discovered that one of the students took the opportunity, being located on the ground floor, to open up an all-night takeaway noodle bar using a water kettle and lots of different flavours of pot noodles.

It made us laugh, and after all, they were catering students! Years later, the college tried to encourage students to set up small businesses, and it was called a student enterprise. Little did we know at that time in Paris, our students were years ahead of the new college initiative.

As with most things, it is good to change the trips, but Paris still seemed an old favourite with our students, so during one year, we decided to stay in the capital of France and take advantage of the city and all its cultural influences. We explored the main attractions and even managed to organise a lunch on the Eiffel Tower and a boat trip on the Seine. On these trips, you are being forced to stay in more traditional accommodations. In my case, I had a wonderful, charming room with the unique feature of being able to sit on the toilet, brush my teeth over the sink, and take a shower all at the same time while most of the lower part of my body was still in the bedroom. All I can say is that I was glad I was not sharing a bedroom on this trip.

I consider myself a very passionate and driven lecturer, but this passion and enthusiasm for your students can sometimes slightly derail one's belief in them as future chefs. We decided on yet another Paris trip to lead the future Escoffier to the Saccreteur and provide our darling with the opportunity to see all over the city whilst exploring a variety of eateries and then make choices about where to take their dinner or, in some cases, their tea. The aim of this exercise was to let the students loose on their own while we enjoyed two hours of culinary delights at the Windmill Restaurant. We arranged to meet the students later that evening, and we were able to exchange all our gastronomic experiences. Amongst others, we were greeted by a very excited student who informed us that because she was in France, she had decided to go all out and eat a typical French meal. We were all very impressed with this statement, as most students would stick to burgers and chips. However, we were less impressed once we learned of the nature of this very typical French meal, which consisted of spaghetti Bolognese.

As for me, I found Paris most inspiring, especially for a pastry chef. On every corner, you will find a patisserie stacked with crispy golden-baked baguettes and flaky, buttery croissants in all varieties, from the simple every day croissant to the ones filled with rich frangipane or chocolate sticks in pain au chocolate.

Many people have heard that the croissant was created in 1686 in Budapest, Hungary, by a courageous, skilled and watchful baker at a time when the city was being attacked by the Turks. Working late one night, they heard odd rumbling noises and alerted the city's military leaders. They found that the Turks were trying to get into the city by tunnelling under the city's walls. The tunnel was destroyed, and the baker was a hero, but a humble hero; all he wanted in reward was the sole right to bake a special pastry commemorating the fight. The pastry was shaped like a crescent, the symbol of Islam, and presumably meant that the Hungarians had eaten the Turks for lunch. The problem with this story is that it is pure fabrication. It first showed up in the first version of the great French food reference Larousse Gastronmique in 1938. Later, the story switched locations to Vienna during the Turkish siege there in 1863, but that was also a tall story. The sad thing is that the truth, in this case, is not nearly as interesting as the myth. No one knows when or where the first croissant was baked, but it was in France and certainly not before 1850. The word was first used in a dictionary in 1863. The first croissant recipe was published in 1891, but it wasn't the same kind of croissant we are familiar with today. The first recipe that would produce what we consider to be a flaky croissant wasn't published until 1905, and, again, it was in France.

Over the years, I worked on several croissant recipes, but I finally came up with a version that I loved best and wanted to share with my students. Nowadays, you will find croissants baked in every corner shop in the UK, but sometimes it is just great to get back to your roots and make your own.

Croissants Page 118

It is hard to resist a good croissant, but a good baguette can also be very tempting. I have stayed many times in France over the years, on trips, with friends, and at a language school. However, I have never seen a baguette that was purchased at the bakery make it to its end destination without the ends being torn off and consumed on its way home.

U p until the 1800s, bread was made with wheat, rye, or buckwheat, and on many occasions, the precious wheat was bulked out with hay, sawdust, mud, or even chalk. Many peasants died from eating this contaminated bread. Many French riots were linked to grain, and bread as rising bread prices made it difficult for poorer families to access bread. In the 19th century, wheat prices were falling, and bread became affordable again, including white bread that, up to this time, was exclusively made for the rich. With the industrial revolution of the early 19th century, steam baking gained popularity in many bakeries across the world. With the addition of the steamed bread, loaves with a crisp crust but an airy interior could be made much more easily. Some believe baguettes were made for Napoleon Bonaparte's soldiers as the long sticks were easier to carry when going into battle. However, it seems more likely that a law passed in the 1920s that prohibited work before 4 a.m. was the reason. Bread loaves, long and thin, needed less time to bake; hence, the baguette was born.

Baguette Page 119

Overall, I consider college trips to be a valuable experience for all involved, as they can enrich, stimulate, and encourage individuals to come out of their shells. On occasions, I see students years later after they have left college, and during our 5-minute exchange on the street, they often bring up the college trips in a nice memory that has stayed with them. I am never sure how I feel when they can't remember how to peel a carrot anymore, but at least they remember their outings during their time at college.

Chapter 6
Commitment and wedding cakes

2004-2010

5.56 a.m., Monday to Friday, was the departure time from the station in south London, which eventually took me to Farnborough, Hampshire, just after 7 a.m. But you still have to get up early, walk to the station, and on arrival, a 15–20-minute walk to the college concludes the commute. I had only completed the first part of my educational journey of becoming a fully qualified lecturer, and with two more years of studying ahead of me, I finally decided to leave London after 10 years of making it my home. It wasn't an easy decision, but deep down, I realised that I had found my calling, and that teaching was the right path for me to be on. The move happened over the summer holidays, so when September finally arrived, it seemed very strange that I could suddenly walk to work. I was in total control of my journey without having to endure train delays, cancellations, or sharing the journey home with drunks.

In the teaching world, we have two starts to a new year. Like everyone else: the first of January but also the 1st of September with the start of the new academic year. I love the rhythm of working from one-half term to the next, making it manageable and hopeful that the next break is not far away. As time went by, I suddenly realised that I had nearly 30 hours of extra time per week to fill by simply not commuting anymore. Boredom has never featured in my life's vocabulary, and after weeks on end of renovating the new house and starting to grow my own fruit and vegetables, I decided to set up a wedding cake business. The initial ideas were sparked by some friends of mine who had asked me to make their wedding cake. After a little research, I finally decided that I would join the army of cakemakers in the local area. From the offset, it was clear to me that the traditional wedding cake was not my bag, and so I opted for the chocolate version of it instead.

As with all humble beginnings, mine started in my relatively small kitchen at my house in Farnborough. After some local advertising and slowly getting to know the wedding venues in my area, the business soon grew despite my rejection of anything other than chocolate. It took me back to the trip to Belgium, where we visited an artisan chocolatier. I remembered how impressed I was with all the beautiful creations he produced in his home. Another dream was about to become reality, complemented by the nightmare of working in a small house kitchen with one fridge, one oven, and a mixer that could only fit onto the draining board. I explored many options on how to upscale the business, moving out of my home kitchen, and after venting my frustration with friends and discussing various options, I finally found the perfect solution: the garage! A double-length garage did not seem the best solution at first, but I had in mind demolishing it to provide the footprint for a new pastry kitchen. After I had further discussion, the space was converted and, to this day, provides a beautiful space away from the house to create all things patisserie and confectionery. The commute is less than 10 seconds from the house, but it does provide the feeling of going to work, genius!

In order to get the most out of the new pastry facilities, I needed to upscale my business, and the only real solution to this was to become an exhibitor at the local wedding fayres. I am talking about the early days of wedding fayres, a special event that provided couples and their friends and families with the opportunity to speak to industry experts. These events were really special, unlike nowadays, where I compare them with a car boot sale that takes place every weekend. Back to the events, I needed to come up with a way to showcase different wedding cakes, but by only using chocolate, it was not at all easy. Eventually, I opted for different-shaped polystyrene cakes that I covered and decorated with carefully tempered, dark, milk and white chocolate, embellished with fresh berries, flowers, or various chocolate decor. This way, I could showcase different styles, and chocolate decorations provided the right aroma the sweet smell of heaven. As with so many wedding cakes, they look amazing, real eyecatchers, but few satisfy when it comes to eating. My sales pitch was always based on the fact that my cake was made with sustainable farm-assured chocolate and not cocoa powder, but the best talk can't beat a real taste test. One of my favourite examples included the white chocolate passionfruit cake, with rich white chocolate and passionfruit truffle filli layered in mouth-watering soft chocolate cake, before being covered in dark chocolate ganache and white chocolate decoration.

Passionfruit White Chocolate Cake Page 121

Despite the fact that I was using high-quality Belgian and Swiss chocolate, it was important to me to share the origin of the chocolate.

At the end of the 19th century and the beginning of the 20th century, well-known UK chocolate producers were fined for using cocoa in products obtained through slavery. Not intentionally, the chocolate factories were run by Quakers, and their principles were based on looking after their workforce and sharing profits. Whole villages were built for chocolate factory workers and their families where they could live but also enjoy life. Unfortunately, much of the cocoa being used came via Portugal, and that was as far as knowledge was shared about the origin of the cocoa beans. Chocolate sales were improving, working conditions were good, and pay was also very competitive. Eventually, questions were raised about the origin of the cocoa beans and where they were grown, as it was common knowledge that cocoa trees do not thrive in Europe. The Portuguese, however, proved to be quite uncooperative, other than revealing that the cocoa was grown in Africa. With that information, the British chocolate makers embarked on their own journey to West Africa and discovered some of the worst working conditions for cocoa farm workers they had ever seen. Many never returned alive after years of abuse and ill-treatment. As they could not resolve the appalling ways the workers were treated, they decided to cut all ties with cocoa farms that were exploiting their work force and find a more humane way of obtaining this raw material. Despite the new-found attitude towards cocoa farmers, many companies were criticised and fined having used cocoa from these plantations. Although their intentions were all well and good now, the fact remained that their success was still built at the cost of human lives.

You see a lot of human life at wedding fayres, a world that up to that point, was unfamiliar to me. I was attending around six fayres a year, three in spring and three in autumn. As weddings are planned not only for months but, in some cases, years ahead, it can't be helped that you see a couple and their entourage for quite some time. I remember one bride-to-be in particular because I had seen her at every wedding fayre I attended. She was always alone, carrying a huge folder of ideas with her, and after a few encounters, she approached me and booked a wedding cake consultation. During a cake consultation, we designed the cake and decided on chocolate flavour options out of the twenty varieties that I offer, followed by a cost for the special cake. As I was finalising the date for the couple to come for their consultation, it suddenly became apparent to me that the bride-to-be not only didn't have a wedding date or venue but, more shockingly, did not have a partner to marry either. She was planning the whole wedding herself with the hope that one day she would meet her Prince Charming so that she could have her perfect wedding. I felt a little sorry for her at first, but after speaking to some of the other exhibitors, I soon discovered she had 'form' and a reputation for being a timewaster.

Like Marie Antoinette, when she said let them eat cake, I found it important to share my cake at wedding fayres regardless of whether someone was getting married or not. On another occasion, I held a consultation for a lovely couple that was due to get married eighteen months later. Finally, the long-planned wedding date had arrived, and when I delivered the cake to the venue, I bumped into the groom. It was not unusual, but it did confuse me, as for the life of me, I could not remember him. I consider myself to have a great memory for people and faces, and this time, it got me, but then again, it was eighteen months ago when I last saw them. The mystery of the unknown groom was later revealed to me by my florist friend, who provided the flowers for the venue and decorated the cake. The reason that I did not recognise the groom was due to the fact that the bride that I met eighteen months ago got rid of her then-boyfriend, the one I met, and replaced him with another one. This change of partner all happened, but her wedding preparation remained in place. The new groom never tasted the cake that I made for his wedding, but I hope he enjoyed the white chocolate coconut and lime cake that he was presented with.

White Chocolate Coconut Lime Cake Page 122

White chocolate is a very controversial type of chocolate, as some believe that because it does not contain cocoa solids and only cocoa butter, it is not real chocolate. Well, in my opinion, it is, as cocoa butter is still derived from the cocoa bean.

There are a variety of stories about the origin of white chocolate, and one of the better-known ones to me is that it was the accidental invention of the German-Swiss chemist Henri Nestle. Nestle was a well-known chocolate producer during the 1930s. He was collaborating with Swiss chocolate maker Daniel Peter to make high-quality milk chocolate. In 1936, however, Nestle teamed up with a pharmaceutical company under the name of Roche, which was developing a tablet named Nestrovit, which was given to children to increase their daily nutrient and vitamin intake. To preserve the tablets from heat and humidity, Nestle provided the cocoa butter that was used for coating the tablets, hence making them fit for purpose.

After some investigation, Nestle created a non-medical version of the tablet by adding sugar, milk, and oil to the cocoa butter and so created the first white chocolate called Galak Bar, better known as 'Milky Bar'.

As with all new businesses, you have to keep evolving, and this is how my next venture took shape, offering a selection of homemade chocolates given by the happy couple to their guests as a symbol of good luck.

This little gift is also known as a wedding favour and can be traced to 16th century England, where the love and good luck symbol was often given in the form of a piece of knotted lace or ribbon. Sugar became more accessible in the 17th century, and despite being mainly used for medicinal purposes, it did make its way to the kitchen, well, at least to the ones who could afford it. Lumps of sugar placed in glass or porcelain boxes decorated with gold, crystals, and gemstones became a popular gift for wedding guests of the aristocracy. These little treasures were eventually named "bonbonniere," and soon the sugar was replaced with beautiful jewels made from chocolate, which were given out to the guests at the wedding of Leopold de Rothschild and Marie Perugia in 1881 in London. Leopold de Rothschild was a British banker born into a wealthy German Jewish banking family, who was also known for his interest in race horse breeding and became the first president of Ealing Football Club, a position he held from 1896-1914. Rothschilds, however, is also a baked almond meringue drizzled in chocolate and together with my mint chocolate crisp tiles, they make a great combination in a wedding favour box.

Rothschild Page 124 & Mint Tiles Page 124

The new pastry kitchen was performing well, but in my initial design, I always envisaged the space being used for teaching passionate individuals like me the art of working with chocolate. It is a tricky skill to get right, requiring practice, patience, and a certain degree of adjustment depending on the type and quality of chocolate. Other things to think about are seasonal temperatures, the humidity level of your working environment, your body temperature, and the type of equipment being used. All these need to be considered when working with chocolate. With all that contemplated, I started to offer chocolate-making courses, from chocolate truffles and pralines to various chocolate decorations.

I always start my courses with a welcome of hot chocolate, as it is this that started the journey of the product we know today.

T he beginning of chocolate can be argued until the cows come home, but I like to link it to around 1500 BC with a tribe called the Olmecs. They were settled in what is now known as Central America. The cocoa beans had their perfect growing conditions, like all areas that sit 10-20 degrees on either side of the equator, but it was only the flesh of the cocoa beans that was of interest to the people of the tribe, as it was sweet, juicy and nutritious. The cocoa bean itself was discarded, probably like what we do when eating fresh cherries: eat the flesh and spit out the pips. Over time, the ground became littered with discarded cocoa beans, and eventually, these beans started to break down as people and animals walked over them. The heat of the sun turned these unassuming beans into something rather nice smelling, like what we now associate with chocolate. It was the Mayans and, later, the Aztecs, who had moved into the area of Mesoamerica around the Gulf of Mexico, who discovered that by grinding and mixing the cocoa beans with water, they could be used as a beverage. The drink was named "Xocolatl," meaning bitter water.

I would like to share with you my version of bitter water with the added indulgence of a little brown sugar.

Aztec Hot Chocolate Page 124

After polishing off the bitter water, we finally enter the well-prepared and laid-out pastry kitchen and start creating beautiful handmade chocolates flavoured with fresh herbs, alcohol, and even mustard. All good chocolates need to undergo a process of tempering by which couverture is made workable so that the end product has a good gloss, a hard surface, a good shelf life, no fat or sugar bloom, and a brittle snap when fractured. I have explained the process of tempering in an earlier chapter, but it can also be found in the recipe section.

Chocolate Tempering Page 125

I was committed to my teaching job and my little wedding cake business, and I enjoyed living in a calmer place than London, but as always, I got this tingling feeling under my feet. Could there be more?

Chapter 7
Competitions, adventures and technology

2010- 2020

It had been nearly seven years of teaching and a long time of studying, and I was still content with my employment. Like so many jobs, technology has accelerated into the work and personal spaces to the point of total reliance. I have always struggled with technology, which is mainly due to a lack of interest on my part, but even I must admit that it has its uses. For instance, it would be hard to imagine writing this diary on a typewriter. When doing a job working with young people, I find it important to see things from their point of view, especially where technology is concerned. As they are used to a different way of learning, I needed to get used to a different way of delivering my teachi. Technology can be a great tool to do that, even for a technophobe like myself.
I used to get quite irritated when I came across a person who simply could not tell the time from an analogue clock. Now, I got over it, as most clocks are digital, and I understand that it might not be as important a skill to have as I remember it to be.

My place of work was full of great work colleagues, and it was rare for people to leave, but it happened, and on one occasion, our team was enriched with a new lecturer. She was full of passion, enthusiasm, and straight-talking, much like myself, except she was British and female. She always saw the good in people, and the very good were encouraged to enter competitions. It is a great way to showcase the college, but the main motivation has always been to build up the learners' already good craft skills as well as improve their confidence levels and self-belief. As there are so many competitions to choose from, it is important to get the right student into the competition that is most suited to them. It could be as simple as decorating a cupcake to show off one's piping skills or shaping bread dough into rolls to demonstrate timing, consistency, and innovation.
Back to my colleague, the female version of myself, who decided to enter a competition named Zest Quest Asia. The competition was founded in 2013 by London-based restaurateurs Cyrus and Pervin Todiwala with the aim of promoting Asian cuisine among British chefs. During the competition, a starter, main course and dessert had to be produced by a team of three. As the main driver of the competition, my colleague identified three student competitors to work on a menu inspired by the culture of Thailand. My role was to support our competitors with the recipe development for the dessert, which included a dish of "lemongrass & salt baked baby pineapple with set coconut cream, kaffir lime sorbet with toasted cashew nuts, and Khanom Kleeb Lamduan." I know it's a bit of a mouthful, but the thinking behind the dishes was based on Thai street food, and the three little desserts fitted that brief. Competition dishes are usually very complex to describe as they require so many little elements. I would, however, like to share the "Khanom Kleep Lamduan," which, in essence, is a Thai shortbread that, once baked, is smoked under a cloche using the traditional candle "Tian Op." In ancient times, this biscuit was strictly to be served to occupants of the Thai palaces but, like so many dishes, eventually made its way to the masses. My research found that the fat used is lard, but in my version, I used vegetable oil. Don't be tempted to use butter, as the biscuit will spread during baking and lose its characteristic flower shape.

Khanom Kleep Lamduan Page 130

A lot of research and training went into the competition, and there was also huge pressure from other college entries. However, our team was not put off by the fact that other competitors had arrived with the most advanced kitchen technology, so how could we compete with a £5 pressure cooker from the charity shop? Well, we did, and on the evening of the competition, the winners were announced, Farnborough College of Technology. These words seem like a distant memory since three young chefs and their lecturers embarked on a trip of a lifetime to Sri Lanka to claim their prize.

Sri Lanka, once known as Ceylon until 1972, welcomed the worthy winners with a respectable 32⁰C and made them comfortable at the Hilton Colombo Hotel. The reception hall was impressive with its large cake and chocolate counter, and our rooms on the 16th floor offered breath-taking views over Sri Lanka's capital, Colombo. After a weekend spent acclimatising to the island, we were all greeted by the HR manager and received a very informative introduction to Sri Lanka as well as the Hilton Hotel group. We learned that almost 140 chefs are employed at the hotel, which was a huge surprise to us all. The day continued with a cookery demonstration at one of the hotel's outdoor restaurant kitchens, 'Curry Leave', where we witnessed and experienced local dishes such as 'Kakukuwo', a crab curry, devilled chicken, and yellow Suduru Samba rice. The whole experience was incredible on its own, but when the Sri Lankan chef arrived and greeted me by my first name, it took me by surprise. After a few exchanged words, I realised that, in fact, our professional paths had crossed at my last job in London, where I was the head pastry chef and he was in charge of breakfast. I did not recognise him at first, but he did, and I felt privileged that he remembered me. The chefs were all very passionate about sharing their local dishes with us, and it was clear from the start that Sri Lankan cuisine is very light, fresh, and flavoursome due to the clever use of spices such as cardamoms, cinnamon, drumstick leaves, lemongrass, chilli, and many more.

Our culinary journey continued with a visit to the local fish market, an unforgettable experience due to its sheer size and hub of activity. Well before sunrise, huge numbers of fish such as sea catfish, tuna, cherry barb, Malabar sprats, green chromide, and lipstick goby changed hands very quickly. The vegetable market in Colombo city centre was equally impressive with its huge piles of fruit, vegetables, and spices, the combined smell of which easily overwhelmed our western nostrils. Roaming the streets of Sri Lanka, we soon came across popular local dishes such as 'hoppers', a basket crafted from a fermented batter made from rice flour and coconut milk filled with eggs, or 'Lunu Miris', a mix of red onion and spices. Other popular dishes included 'Pittu', a cylinder of steamed rice mixed with grated coconut, and 'Kevum', a sweet rice flour-based deep-fried oil cake. Back at the hotel, we were fortunate enough to learn how to prepare and cook these dishes. Impressed with our excitement for the local gastronomy, one of the chefs went out to the market to purchase an array of specialised cooking utensils so that we could make the new dishes back home in England. Armed with a Sri Lankan cookery book and a vast collection of local kitchen gadgets, we felt ready to take on the challenge and introduce Sri Lankan foods to our menu at the college. A local Sri Lankan food supplier had already been found back in the UK.

One cannot visit Sri Lanka and not talk about tea, but what we were about to experience and learn about Sri Lanka's tea changed my views of tea forever. A three-hour bus journey from Columbo took us to the Rilhena Estate, one of many belongings of the Dilmah dynasty. We learned that tea in its simple form grows in three main regions in Sri Lanka from low-grown, mid-grown to high-grown.

The Rilhena estate was constructed in 1914, is located at an elevation of 153 metres above sea level, and is therefore considered as low growing. The owner, Merrill J. Fernando, a man of extraordinary vision, strength, and integrity, was finally in a position in 1988 to set up his dream of his own plantation. He founded the Dilmah Estate, which now consists of over 30 estates across Sri Lanka. He believes in family values and business as a matter of human service, and with his knowledge and inspiring passion for tea, he can produce artisanal, handmade traditional tea. After gaining insight into growing, harvesting, and processing tea, it became very apparent that Merill J. Fernando's vision was not just about tea. To him, it was equally important to support the underprivileged and marginalised communities by providing a huge variety of projects. They include housing and building communities, mid-day meal programmes, school bags for plantation children, healthcare and medical camps, as well as a huge number of small entrepreneurial programmes for his workers. In addition, he is providing opportunities for the differently-abled, women's empowerment, as well as conserving nature, natural resources, and cultural diversity.

Our tea journey continued with a twelve-course taster menu where we were challenged to sample a selection of foods with different teas. Rather like matching food with wine, the tea becomes the perfect accompaniment to the dishes. Some of the combinations were beef burgers with Earl Grey tea, pork sausage with Darjeeling, and sea bass with green tea. Desserts on offer included apple pie with camomile and dark chocolate with Ceylon Souchong, a speciality tea smoked with cinnamon bark. I consider Sri Lanka as a trip of a lifetime and feel immensely privileged that we were able to experience fragments of a truly fascinating country with all its cultural heritage and local gastronomy. One of these foods included a tropical fruit native to Southeast Asia, including Sri Lanka, called wood apple. The wood apple, commonly known as Bael fruit, grows on a tree-like plant and is similar to a quince. The high pectin content makes it an ideal candidate to be used in jam making, which is included in my 'no-yeast' doughnut recipe.

Wood Apple Doughnuts Page 130

When I started my professional career in 1986, it was always drummed into me that France was the godfather of all food creations, the centre of classical cooking full of inspiration and innovation. On the other hand, when asked about British food, the first thing that came to mind was "brown food." Well, how have things changed? I personally feel that French cuisine has been resting on its laurels, but food in Britain has taken the world by storm. Through hard work, passion, and determination, but most of all, by creating a new identity through a new form of food created by its vast cultural diversity. Learning from different cultures has always fascinated me, but when you are able to combine it with something that is already familiar, it becomes truly magical.

In 2016, I found myself very fortunate to visit the island of Jamaica. Partly to visit family in the town of Brownstown, but also with the aim of learning about the cocoa and spice production of the Sun Valley Plantation near Ocho Rios. A full-working family plantation run by Lorna and Nolly Binns offered a truly sensational opportunity to explore their stunning gardens, full of different fruits, spices, and cocoa trees, which were used either for culinary or medicinal purposes. The plantation had been in the family for over 250 years, and the main crop used to be bananas, but in order to create a wind barrier between the banana trees, they also planted coconut trees. Little did they know that eventually, the coconuts produced from the wind barrier trees were the start of their coconut water business, which they officially launched in 1996. Young jelly coconuts are harvested after eight months because of their abundance of water. After being shown how to harvest them by one of the plantation workers, we were able to drink the clear, slightly sweet liquid that poured out of these young coconuts. Simply delicious-but also a newly found respect for the growers.

An array of spices is grown on the plantation, too, from cinnamon to nutmeg and mace to Jamaican pimento, also known as allspice. As we were shown around the plantation, I noticed many green-looking beans hanging from some of the trees, and after some discussions, I learned, in fact, that these green beans were vanilla pods. My initial enthusiasm was soon saddened when Lorna told me that all of the vanilla beans had to be hand pollinated as they had lost all of the pollinating bees. She gave me a toothpick, and I spent the next hour hand-pollinating vanilla beans, something everyone should do before moaning about the price of them. In honour of Lorna and Nollie Binns, I designed a vanilla and coconut set cream served with my coconut tile biscuits to say thank you for an amazing experience and for their inspiration for growing such beautiful ingredients.

Vanilla Coconut Panna Cotta & Coconut Tiles Page 131

I found myself very fortunate that I grew up in Germany, a country where I had the choice of training as a chef or a pastry chef, despite not knowing the pastry training option available to me back in the late 1980s. In my opinion, it is a good route to train as a chef and then specialise in patisserie. At my place of work at the college, we had always adopted this way of training young people. Setting solid foundations in all areas of hospitality before choosing a personal route. But on some occasions, you do come across a passionate individual who just knows that they want to become a pastry chef, and our response was always to reject and squash their dream with a no and a sorry that we do not offer this way of learning. However, once you have gutted fish and cut up chickens and have been a waiter to hundreds of customers for nearly two years, then you can become a pastry chef. Not really selling it, is it?

Television shows might have been the catalyst in sparking the huge interest in baking and making cake, and if that is the case, I am all for it. Not exactly a new invention being influenced by the media, but with everyone having access to their own broadcasting devices, you don't have to agree on what to watch collectively.

This could be the reason that cookery programmes have gained mass popularity since they were first televised in November 1936 on the BBC. A cook, under the name of Rosina Dixon, showed viewers how to roll out pastry while singing, insisting that her musical interludes would keep the pastry light.

If you repeat things enough times, people start to believe them, or as Napoleon Bonaparte is reported to have said, "history is a series of events of the things that people remember," which implies not always being true. I am not convinced that singing makes pastry light, but it certainly won't harm it.

Early television broadcasting would have had a very different audience from the ones that listen to radio. For one, if you could afford to have a television, it would have been unlikely you did the cooking yourself, making cooking programmes kind of pointless. The ones that were broadcast tended to be more for entertainment purposes rather than being copied hands-on. In contrast, radios became much more accessible to people who actually worked in kitchens, so many recipes were exchanged this way. Shortly after the cooking singing sensation appeared on the BBC, another cook, Moira Meighn, presented a cookery programme called "Quarter of an Hour Meals". The aim was to showcase the use of simple kitchen equipment when preparing wholesome foods. 1937 started the year with chef Xavier Marcel Boulestine, a cookery show named "Cooks' Night Out," where, over five episodes, one dish was created and, when put together, would make up a five-course meal. Several short timeslots to present culinary skills were broadcasted between 1937 and 1939, but due to WWII, these came to a sharp end when, on the 1st of September 1939, the BBC broadcasting was shut down in England.

After the war, chef Philip Harben demonstrated a 10-minute-long programme where he showed viewers how to make lobster vol-au-vents. Controversial in so many ways, not only making a dish using lobster despite ongoing rationing shortly after the war but also his move to television from radio, where he had presented previous food programs. 1947 saw English home economist and wartime food consultant Marguerite Patten demonstrate cooking expertise aimed at women alongside her job at Harrods, where, after the war, she was hired to demonstrate cooking appliances such as refrigerators, stoves, and pressure cookers.

Fanny Cradock took the nation by storm in 1955 with her programme "Kitchen Magic," where she aimed to bring fine French foods to the British home. One of her creations was the Ambassador cake, which isn't really a cake at all and, in my view, more like a chocolate dessert.

I have adapted Fanny's recipe to make it mine, but the original recipe can be found on the internet.

Ambassador Cake Page 132

In 1973, Delia Smith appeared on TV with her cookery programme 'Family Fayre', where her focus was on step-by-step instructions for creating English classics. She was so influential that her audience took everything she said as gospel, which led to empty supermarket shelves once she had recommended a certain ingredient or a certain size cake tin. With no social media at the time, she remained relatively unknown to the rest of the world. The 1980s saw a real explosion in the culinary world when the BBC introduced the "Food and Drink" programme, hosted by Simon Bates and Gillian Milles. It also paved the way for wine expert Jilly Goolden, well known for her overuse of adjectives when describing her wines; you could almost taste them. Madhur Jaffrey, a TV personality and food writer, brought Indian cookery to English speakers in 1982, opening a real insight into another culture; food suddenly came alive with an array of spices and colours. As mentioned earlier in the book, I arrived in the UK in 1994, but it was also the year when the late Gary Rhodes launched his TV series "Rhodes about Britain."

A very good friend of mine worked for him in the pastry kitchen at his restaurant in London, where she invited me to spend the day with her as part of my professional development. Here, we made his perfect lemon posset with shortbread.

Lemon Posset & Short Bread Page 132

I do believe that Gary Rhodes was a leader when it came to inspiring young chefs, but many followed, including Ainsley Harriot in 1997 with 'Ainsley's Barbecue Bible,' Hugh Fernley Whittingstall 'Cook on the Wild' followed closely by Gordon Ramsay's 'Boiling Point' show and Nigel Slater's 'Real Food Show' both aired in 1998. The millennium saw Nigella Lawson bring food back to the home kitchen with the 'Nigella Bites' series, followed by many more.

Cooking and baking have now been accepted as well-regarded job choices, whereas up to this point, they were seen to make a living for young people who did not do well at school. During the first half of the millennium, television and social media platforms became saturated, but there was still room for one new invention towards the end of the first decade of the new century. On the 17th of August 2010, ten home bakers were put together in a show to bake against each other, and after weeks of battling it out, the first winner of 'The Great British Bake Off' was announced. The programme has been running ever since, and in 2016, a version for professional pastry chefs was launched.

With so much publicity about pastry chefs and pasty cooking, we finally managed to run our first patisserie course for school leavers at Farnborough College in 2017. Two years later, this was offered to day-release part-time students, consisting mostly of adults with a strong passion for pastry cooking. Pastry courses are based on a serious of skill-building tasks, that are tested at regular intervals with an assessment and followed by a final exam. Two of the dishes that I must assess on a regular basis during the final exam are Swiss sponge roulade filled with crème mousseline and the classic chocolate fondant.

It would be an obvious assumption that the Swiss roll sponge roulade was created in Switzerland, but this thin sponge, which is baked at high heat for a short time to retain its moisture, has been traced to 19th century central Europe, possibly Austria. A version of the Swiss roll can also be found in America, where it is known as jelly roll, where the jelly is spread quickly over the just baked sponge before being rolled up into a cloth and allowed to set.

45

My mother still uses cloth today, which she sprinkles liberally with caster sugar before tipping the baked sponge roulade onto it and rolling it up. The cloth is used to trap the steam that is released from the cooling sponge, helping to retain moisture and, therefore, making it easier to roll. For my students, the use of a cloth is banned because a perfectly baked Swiss sponge roulade should roll up without the use of a cloth.

Many nations have taken the 19th-century invention and created their own version. In Germany, they are known as the 'Bisquitrolle', often filled with lemon or strawberry cream. Japanese and Chinese pastry chefs use whipped cream and strawberries, coffee, or oranges to prepare rolled sponges sold alongside local delicacies. Indonesia called theirs 'Bolu Gulung' where a filling of cheese or, more traditionally, buttercream and jam can be found. In 1931, India started to make jam rolls filled with pineapple and strawberries and named them 'Kunjus'. Even the Italians liked this light and fluffy sponge roulade but added cocoa powder to make a chocolate Swiss roll sponge before being packed full of ricotta cheese and marzipan and named it 'Rollo'. In the UK, simple strawberry jam is used before rolling up and lightly dusting in icing sugar, but for my student's final exam, I expect a filling of crème mousseline, a type of buttercream based on a set custard and butter.

Swiss Roll & Crème Mousseline Page 133

For my second recipe, I would like to share with you a classic chocolate fondant, which some regard as an under-baked pudding.

Research has revealed that this French classic was invented by French Michelin star chef Michel Bras as recently as 1981. Known as 'Fondant au Chocolat' meaning melted chocolate, which is achieved by baking it at a high temperature for a short time, and if done correctly, the soft centre should be held in place by a crisp exterior. There is, however, a more romantic story attached to this luscious, sweet treat where a pastry chef falls in love with a girl from a rich family in Paris. As his social status was not superior enough to marry her, the girl's parents arranged for her to marry the son of a Duke. The young pastry chef, still in love with the girl, was asked to make the dessert for the wedding banquet and created the 'fondant au chocolat'. The groom and all the guests loved his creation, but the bride was brought to tears as she was the only one who could understand that the melting centre represented the hot love she felt towards her beloved pastry chef.

When making this dish, it can be a love-hate relationship as it can be a tricky dessert to get right, so I do turn a blind eye to the occasional swear word passing my students' lips-well at least during the practice lessons.

Chocolate Fondant Page 134

It was going so well, but then we were all thrown into a state of panic, uncertainty, upset, and, quite frankly a terrifying situation called COVID 19. How could this happen in the 21st century?

There had been so many world events that devastated our ancestors, including the 'Plague of Justinian', a disease spread by infected rats on merchant ships in 541AD. The 'Black Death' killed half of Europe's population between 1347 and 1353 but then resurfaced again in 1629 as the Italian plague. London was not spared horrible diseases and felt the brunt of them during the 16th and 17th centuries, and in 1720, the great plague of Marseille took many lives, too. The 'Third Plague Pandemic' erupted in China in 1855, closely followed by the Spanish flu in 1918.

These historical events that we know only from history books suddenly creep up on us, and before you know it, you are part of history. We got a small taster in 2009 when the Swine Flu swept the UK, and at that time, we created learning packs for our students, which were great, but unfortunately, they were all theory based, which can be tricky for practical-minded students and lecturers. So, back to COVID-19, with little notice, all our lives, including education and training, were thrown into chaos, but with one little addition that made all the difference: technology. Like so many of us, we knew and used a bit of it already, but the situation we were finding ourselves in accelerated the implementation of technology into our daily lives. It started off with team calls where we could meet with colleagues and students. Not only were we able to keep an eye on everything, but this way, we could establish a routine, which, in my opinion, is vital to keeping a healthy state of mind. The next step involved getting students to cook and bake at home, but with some food shortages, it was quite a tricky task to master at times. Not to be defeated, I converted my pastry kitchen at home into a live-streaming baking environment, and I started to demonstrate a variety of bakes to my students.

Previously, my pastry kitchen was used to create wedding cakes, but as no one could get married, it seemed the perfect solution to keep my kitchen alive. Now, one can think that it is not a million miles away from what I do at college; after all, I demonstrate dishes all the time. So wrong; not only did I have to demonstrate how to make my chosen bakes, but I had to keep them going and interlink them with other dishes so that a smooth delivery could be guaranteed. In a normal college setting, after a demonstration, the students would go off and recreate what they had watched. In this situation, all eyes were on me, so it required much more than deciding which dishes to bake. With that in mind, very detailed plans were devised and executed with military precision. One of the bakes that made the cut was macarons, something my level 3 students would have to make during their final exam. These fluffy pillow-like meringues are easily confused with mountains of coconut and egg whites dipped in chocolate, known as macaroons, using two o's in the spelling of them. I used to bake these with my grandmother in the early 1970s.

However, the macarons are believed to have started life in 1792 in the French city of Nancy, where two Carmelite nuns became known as the 'Macaron Sisters'. In 1952, the two nuns were honoured by the city of Nancy by renaming the place where the sisters made the macarons after them. These traditional petit fours have naturally evolved over the years, and these two meringue halves have been sandwiched together with all sorts of fillings, including many savoury ones. They became very fashionable during the 1830s in Paris, and the famous Parisienne patisserie 'Ladurée', which opened in Paris in 1862, reintroduced them as 'macaron Parisienne'. At the beginning of the 21st century, they once again increased in popularity, and in 2005, the French pastry chef Pierre Hermé introduced Macaron Day, which is now celebrated on the 20th of March each year.

Apart from the many fillings found inside the macaron, there are three potential ways to make the shells. Version one, known as the Italian method, involves making a meringue by whisking hot sugar syrup into egg whites before folding in ground almonds and icing sugar. Another way to make them is the French method, where egg whites are whisked up before adding sugar slowly. Alternatively, Swiss meringue is used when warming sugar and egg whites in a water bath before whisking into a foam. Now, I will give you a choice of which one you want to try and bake, and for this purpose, I would like to share my macaron bible.

Macaron Bible Page 135-139

It was great to receive so many pictures of my students' macarons, or at least the attempts at them, but don't get disheartened if you can't get them right the first time; keep trying, and you will get there.

For my lower-level students, I decided to show them how to make Welsh cakes.

A combination of flour, fats, sugar, and dried fruit, they became popular towards the end of the 19th century. They are baked on a griddle and, in Wales, are often referred to as bakestones. A combination of a biscuit and a scone, these tasty treats are enjoyed hot or cold. I eat mine while still warm, smothered with clotted cream and a good dollop of homemade strawberry jam. I know, very indulgent, but I'm worth it. Traditionally, these cakes were given to the Welsh coal miners as their stable texture would make them ideal to be pocketed into a jacket without breaking. Welsh schoolchildren might also find them in their lunchboxes, and they are a must in Wales when having an afternoon tea. Nowadays, you find all sorts of different nuts, fruits, seeds, or even cheese inside them.

Welsh Cakes Page 140

The pandemic also had a huge impact on travel, and this was one of the reasons that I wanted to share recipes that were linked to the British Isles. Relatively unknown in the south of the UK, I decided to share my "Parkin" recipe, a popular cake found in the north and in and around Yorkshire.

One of the reasons I like this cake is because of its name, Parkin, a popular surname in the north of England meaning Peter. It is also my mother's maiden name, except hers has an s at the end and reads Peters. A far-fetched link, I know, but to me, Parkin means mother, and you have to hold on to whatever you can when, like me, you live in a foreign country without blood relations, and this is a lovely reminder of my beautiful mum.

Back to the Parkin, this slightly sticky ginger cake full of treacle and brown sugar is usually made and eaten on bonfire night, more commonly known as Guy Fawkes Night. Fireworks displayed all over the UK light up the sky and celebrate the capture of Guy Fawkes, who attempted, on the 5th of November 1605, to blow up the Houses of Parliament in London with the aim of assassinating King James I of England. The gunpowder plot was one of many attempts to kill the king, and as Guy Fawkes was caught red-handed with numerous barrels of explosives under the House of Lords, we now associate the 5th of November with him. The truth, however, is that the ringleader of the king's assassination attempt was a man by the name of Robert Catesby.

It always fascinates me how historical events are linked to foods, even if the event happened much earlier than the food it is associated with.

During the industrial revolution of the mid-18th century, oats and treacle were common ingredients for the working classes, and so many Parkin recipes can be found from 1760 onwards. Lancashire Parkin is similar to Yorkshire Parkin, except it does not contain oats.

When I first started to research parkin recipes, I noticed that parkin was made with black treacle, and some versions used golden syrup. Black treacle and golden syrup are, in their basic form, the same thing: sugar. Black treacle is, of course, much darker in colour, stronger, and bitter in flavour, and, according to real die-hard parkin fans, a must-have ingredient when making a proper parkin. I made both versions, and for myself, I decided to use a recipe that uses black treacle and golden syrup. Apologies to all die-hard Parkin fans! However, I do adopt the parkin etiquette that a good parkin must not be eaten on the day of being baked, even if the smell drives you crazy. Leave it for at least a couple of days so that the flavours and stickiness in the cake can develop and, therefore, deliver maximum enjoyment.

Parkin Page 141

Sticking with the British traditional bakes for my next lockdown demonstration, I decided to share a version of the classic Battenberg Cake.

Again, my choice might have been influenced by the British-German connection as, historically, this bake is linked to the marriage celebration of Queen Victoria's granddaughter, Princess Victoria, to German-born Prince Louis of Battenberg in 1884. The German town of Battenberg, located in the German county of Hessen, was given its name by the Battenberg family, which had a royal link to the house of "Hesse-Darmstadt." The intention of the cake's creation was to link British and German tastes together in this rather simple jam-sandwiched cake covered in marzipan. The formation of the four equal squares in the cake represents the four princes of Battenberg but is also a nod to the German rococo architecture. Interestingly enough, to this day, the checkerboard patterns seen on the front of emergency vehicles are referred to as Battenberg markings. In Europe, Germany was seen as the capital of marzipan, and apart from providing sweetness to the sandwiched cake squares, the wrap-around almond covering will keep the cake fresh for longer. In my personal view, the checkerboard pattern, traditionally pink and yellow, is a perfect example of the bringing together of two. It also represents equality, something rather absent at the time of this creation, but in my mind, it represents just that: equality! Other names for similar-looking cakes are 'Domino Cake', 'Neapolitan Roll', or 'Church Window Cake'.

For my version of this classic, I have chosen the flavours of rose and almond cakes sandwiched with rosewater-flavoured apricot jam before being hidden under a blanket of marzipan.

Battenberg Cake Page 141

We are now living with COVID, and many parts of our lives have restarted. So, many of us have gone back to what we knew before, but one thing is for sure: during and after the pandemic, technology has accelerated all lives. In essence, this has provided more flexibility in how we work, where we work, and so on. Most importantly, many of us have started to bake and have developed a new appreciation for patisserie and confectionery, which, in my mind, is a little ray of sunshine after such a horrible time.

Chapter 8
Pop-up, teas and the Jamaican story garden

2020- 2023

The year 2022 marked my twentieth anniversary of teaching at the technology college, and despite my passion and enthusiasm for my work, colleagues, and students, time takes its toll. For a few years now, I have been reducing my work commitments at the college to three days per week. Despite having no plans to slow down, I wanted a different pattern of life. When I first started my three-day working week at the college, I was overcome with guilt when going for walks on midweek mornings and trying desperately to justify my day when people asked me what I did all day. After a while, it became easier, and I felt more comfortable with the decisions that I had made. I also needed the time to figure out how to create a different pattern for my existence. People who know me are fully aware that I have a strong interest in interior design, upcycling, and repurposing all kinds of objects and hand-me-downs. In my mind, all I had to do was to apply this concept to my own life and utilise and fill the time that was given to me with more than one set of rules, and the answer presented itself: setting up a pop-up café.

The initial idea came from a friend of mine with whom I hosted a couple of pop-up dinner events at a local guest house. After that, I set up a pop-up café in a furniture restoration shop, and this was the beginning of establishing a client base. COVID put a stop to that, but after the lockdown, I decided it would be far easier to host pop-up events from my house, and so the first seed was planted, well, at least in my head. Talking about planting, the front of our house was already a well-established tropical garden. It was designed, planted up, and cared for by my long-life soul mate and partner of mixed-race Jamaican descent. However, during lockdown, the garden took on a whole new dimension when a waterfall and river were created on what was the front wall. The raised river was further embellished with a large bridge and roof structure entirely made from bamboo and string. The whole scene came to life with handmade figures displaying a fully working Jamaican community. Apart from a love for tropical plants, one of the aims of the Jamaican Story Garden was to share the rich cultural heritage through the mediums of storytelling, gardening, and sculpture.

According to my research, the island of Jamaica was first discovered by the explorer Christopher Columbus on May 4th 1494. Columbus claimed the island for the King and Queen of Spain, and its colonisation began. When the Spanish first arrived on the island, it was populated by a race of people known as Arawaks or Tainos. These gentle people had mostly likely settled on the island from the country now known as Guyana, where Arawak Indians can still be found today. The Spaniards made the Arawaks into slaves and treated them so harshly that within fifty years, nearly all the Arawaks were dead. The Spaniards then replaced them with slaves from Africa.

Towards the end of lockdown, the Jamaican Story Garden was discovered by locals and soon gained in popularity. We ended up with a gold medal for the best front garden and another one for attracting wildlife, both awarded by the local council. Social media and word of mouth spread like wildfire, and "The Jamaican Story Garden" started to draw in the crowds. We met so many lovely people who were full of compliments, and most conversations ended with, "Where can I go for a cup of tea and a piece of cake around here?" After a while, I took these comments as a sign and opened the garden gate, baked a few cakes, and put the kettle on for anyone who wanted to come in. One of the first cakes that we offered our visitors was a lemon drizzle cake. I had just baked it when I got chatting to some strangers in the front garden, and the next minute, we were all perched on the garden wall enjoying the cake.

Not knowing for sure how this British favourite came about, some believe that a Jewish woman named Evelyn Rose made a version of lemon drizzle cake in 1967. What makes this cake different is that once it's baked, it is brushed with lemon juice and sugar, which is the 'drizzle' in the lemon drizzle cake.

I make my version with ground almonds, but you can replace these with flour if you wish.

Lemon Drizzle Cake Page 146

The concept of a pop-up café was relatively unknown in our area, but nationally, you could see a surge in demand for this unusual venture. The idea of supper clubs seems to have American roots as far back as the 1930s, and these places were often found at the edge of a town where simple food and entertainment were offered. In the United Kingdom, the concept of supper clubs was soon to follow suit, with the aim of offering good food in an informal setting. The British supper clubs were places where people brought their own wine, too. Another important feature of the supper clubs is that, unlike in a restaurant, you would share tables with total strangers, something I found very appealing when thinking about my own pop-up venture.

Don't get me wrong, the theory of a pop-up is very simple, but a successful one is based on hard work. You can't just open your house or garden and expect people to turn up, so do your groundwork, and over time, things will come together. If you are in it purely for the money, forget it, as there are much easier ways to do that. As with all things, I believe that whatever you do, you need heart, and liking people helps, too. We had the destination as our unique selling point with the garden, and I knew how to make a cake or two. With my strong background in interior and exterior design, "The Jamaican Story Garden" pop-up café was established. One of the cakes that people expect to see on the menu now is my own invention of the hummingbird cake, which is based on a white chocolate and coconut lime cake topped with white chocolate and mango truffle mousse before being topped with fresh pineapple, mango, and passion fruit syrup.

The hummingbird in Jamaica, also known as "The Doctor Bird" or "Swallow Tail Hummingbird," is one of over 300 species of hummingbirds, but this one only exists in Jamaica, and that was the reason I wanted to create a cake to celebrate this national bird of Jamaica.

Jamaican Story Garden Hummingbird Cake Page 144

Another Caribbean treat that is on offer is the Jamaican bun.

Strongly linked to the British hot cross bun, the Jamaican bun and cheese is also a traditional dish eaten during the Easter period. Brought to Jamaica by the British when they colonised the island in the middle of the 17th century, the hot cross bun has been modified over time by the indigenous inhabitants of Jamaica by adding cinnamon, pimento, nutmeg, and molasses, as well as eating it with orange Tastee cheese. The hot cross bun, which symbolised the crucifixion of Jesus Christ, was well known by Jamaicans, and many of them grew up singing the hot cross bun nursery rhyme.

Hot cross buns!

Hot cross buns!

One a penny, two a penny,

Hot cross buns!

If you have no daughters,

Give them to your sons.

One a penny, two a penny,

Hot cross buns!

Jamaican Bun Page 146

As with all types of cafés, you have to offer drinks, and as coffee is becoming very popular in the UK, I decided to keep the coffee offerings simple. I know the total opposite of what is on trend. It has always been in my DNA to go with my instinct rather than follow the crowds or trends, and many times, this did not work in my favour. However, on this occasion, I decided to stick to my guns and make tea and hot chocolate, the star attraction drinks, rather than coffee.

One of my main reasons for this was sparked by a memory that resurfaced about an experience that I had on the island of Sri Lanka. Here, I was fortunate to visit and encounter the joy of being in a tea lounge, and I was overcome by the beautiful aroma of the tea. Then again, I love the smell of coffee too, so I thought a coffee bar does sell tea, so what is the big deal? Well, let me tell you, a tea lounge is a very peaceful place, as the pouring of gently bubbling water that is trickled over tea is hardly noticeable. In stark contrast to the grinding of coffee beans, the steam gushing and slapping of pots onto the counter you get from a full-blown barista experience. It was a no-brainer to focus on tea!

When preparing a drink in a quiet and calm fashion, the whole atmosphere becomes almost tranquilising as visitors talk much more calmly to each other and are more likely to switch their phones off and embrace these moments of cathedral-like contemplation. As soon as you enter a coffee bar, you are greeted by the noise created by the drink's preparation, which automatically ends up with visitors raising their voices. I knew which environment I wanted to create, so the cafetières were ready for coffee lovers and had a large selection of tea for the rest. This way, they would all benefit from a gentle preparation method, all contributing to the calm and peaceful environment I wanted for my visitors.

Before sharing my tea journey, I would like to mention a special coffee-flavoured cake known as the "Gateau Opera," which, strangely, is a firm favourite with my tea-drinking customers. This famous gateau constructed of thin almond sponges, also known as "Jaconde," is perfumed with rum and layered with silky smooth coffee-flavoured buttercream before being topped with chocolate ganache. The design of this delicious treat was with the intention that, with every mouthful, you would enjoy the same ratio of each layer.

The origin of the opera has been linked to two patisseries in France. The pastry chef Cyriaque Gavillon, who worked for the Maison Dalloyau, claimed his invention in 1955. He goes on further and affirms that his wife Andrée Gavillon gave the cake its name, as his creation was in tribute to the Opera House Garnier. Some believe the cake was named as a salute to the dancers of the opera house who frequently visited the pastry shop. Another claimant to this coffee-flavoured invention is Gaston Lenôtre, the founder of the patisserie Maison Lenôtre, who made his invention known in the 1960s.

My recipe for the classic 'Gateau Opera' has also evolved over time, and I ended up with an Italian buttercream in my version of this French classic. Apologies to the French inventors!

Opera Page 147

I am often asked about the difference between all the buttercreams. They all contain sugar and butter; they have different characteristics, skill challenges and, of course, different flavour profiles and mouthfeel. Most bakers make butter icing by simply combining icing sugar with butter. The French version is made with an egg foam slowly beaten into butter, whereas the Germans incorporate custard in butter, which I listed how to make in my crème mousseline recipe. Russian combines condensed milk with butter, and in my Italian buttercream recipe, this smooth, silky texture is achieved by beating Italian meringue into butter. I like all of them, and it is down to personal preferences on which to use.

Back to my discovery of tea, I knew that to be a successful pop-up, you must go the extra mile. Rather than simply offering a cup of builder's tea, the odd Earl Grey, or herb and fruit infusions, I wanted to make the drinks as important as the cakes and be a contributor to the whole Jamaican Story Garden experience.

My research into tea has revealed that there are over 3000 teas made from different varieties of tea plants, and somehow, like wine, they differ greatly in their character, colour, and flavour. These all depend on many factors, such as where the tea is grown, including altitude and climate, seasonal changes, cultivation and harvesting methods, tea leaf processing, storage, and transport, as well as the way the tea is brewed.

Tea has long been produced in China, India, Africa, South America, and even Europe, but it seemed like a mammoth process to decide what teas I could offer. I wanted to get it right, so I decided to embark on my own tea journey, which I would like to share in this diary. My first task was to write a tea menu that offers a wide variety of teas from different tea groups, and I found the following groups that I wanted to explore a little more.

The first group I learned more about was white tea, which is named after the tiny white, silvery hairs that cover the bud at the tip of each shoot. It's produced on a very limited scale, and although originally from China, it is also now produced in Sri Lanka. After steaming, the buds are dried and then shaped. White teas are champagne coloured and have a light, sweet, and velvety flavour. The caffeine content, which is negligible, is the lowest of all tea types.

The yellow teas are China's rarest and are similar to white teas. New buds are left in piles to oxidise. The heat caused during this process dries them out, thus preventing further decomposition. When brewed, they give a pale yellow and greenish liquor with a delicate sweetness. Yellow tea has more caffeine than most green teas.

Green tea is often referred to as 'unoxidized' or 'non-fermented'. Processing differs by region but is based on similar principles. Freshly picked leaves are withered (left out to dry) and then heat treated. In China, the traditional method is still employed. Leaves are spread out and exposed to sunlight or warm air for a couple of hours before being placed into hot roasting pans. This makes the leaves soft and moist and allows the moisture to evaporate. After a few minutes, the leaves are placed on bamboo tables and rolled. Once rolled, the balls are placed into the hot roasting pans for a second time before being rolled again. After one or two hours, the leaves turn a dull green colour and undergo no further changes. At this stage, the leaves are sieved to separate them by size.

An unusual tea variety I discovered is the oolong teas, which are generally known as 'semi-fermented' or 'semi-oxidised' and are traditionally the products of China and Taiwan. To give oolong teas their rich flavour, the leaves are picked near their peak and processed immediately after plucking. The leaves are first wilted in warm air or direct sunlight and are then shaken in bamboo baskets to lightly bruise the edges of the leaves. This fermentation, or oxidation period normally takes 1½ hours and is halted by firing once the surface of the leaves is yellow and the edges are a reddish colour. Oolongs are whole-leaf teas and are not broken by rolling.

The production of black teas varies considerably by region, but the process always involves four basic stages: withering, rolling, oxidation (fermentation), and drying (firing). The two major processing methods are 'orthodox' and 'CTC' (cut, tear and curl method). In the traditional method, the leaves are spread out in warm air and allowed to wither until they're soft enough to roll without the surface of the leaf splitting. Next, the leaves are rolled in order to release the chemicals required for oxidation. Although this is sometimes done by hand, rotorvane machines that lightly crush the leaf are normally used. The rolled lumps of a leaf are then left in cool, humid atmospheric conditions for up to 4 hours to absorb oxygen. The chemical change in the leaves turns them from green to a coppery red colour. The final stage requires the leaf to be oxidised or fermented to prevent natural decomposition. At this stage, the leaves turn black and are recognisable as tea. The Cut Tear Curl method is widely used in the production of black tea and produces smaller particles that give a stronger, quicker brew, ideal for use in tea bags. The leaf is withered in the same way, but instead of being rolled, it's passed through the rollers of a CTC machine, which rotate at different speeds, or in a Lawrie Tea Processor (LTP) rotating hammer-mill leaf disintegrator, which tears and breaks the leaf into tiny particles. The remaining oxidation and drying stages are the same as the orthodox method. After discovering such large varieties of tea to choose from, I noticed that there was still one group of teas missing, which I wanted to include in my pop-up tea menu. The teas I am talking about here are the ones made from herbs, fruit, or bark, also known as tisane tea. So, a classic mint and summer berry, as well as a rooibos tea, made it onto my tea menu, as all of these teas are naturally caffeine-free.

Still not out of the woods, I needed to decide which type of white, black, green, or oolong tea I wanted to offer. After some market research, the following tea varieties are now available for everyone to enjoy at the pop-up café:

Black Teas:

Breakfast Tea
A blend of black tea from Assam, Ceylon, and Kenya. Strong and full-bodied, robust, and rich in flavour, it goes well with milk and sugar.

Earl Grey Tea
Made from a blend of black teas, including Chinese Keemun black tea with its stony and woody notes. Earl Grey is flavoured with citrus and bergamot and can be enjoyed with either milk or fresh lemon. A decaffeinated version is also available.

Darjeeling Tea
An Indian black tea with a fruity, floral, and muscatel aroma. I recommend this tea without milk or sugar, but you are welcome to have it. Fresh lemon could also be an option.

Lapsang Souchong Tea
A Chinese smoked black tea. Souchong refers to the fourth and fifth leaves of the tea plant, which are coarser in texture, making them stronger when smoked over pinewood. Recommend without milk, but some like to have milk with it. Sugar is not normally added to this tea, but the choice is yours.

Assam Tea
This Indian black tea, with its brisk and malty flavour profile, is best enjoyed without milk, but some like it with sugar as it can counterbalances the slight bitterness.

Green Teas
I serve Chinese green teas made from the evergreen shrub "Camellia Sinensis." These sweet to bittersweet nutty teas are best enjoyed without milk but might be sweetened. I offer plain green tea, jasmine green tea with a bitter floral scent, as well as rose green tea with a sweet floral aroma.

Oolong Tea
Also known as dark green tea, it is similar to green tea but has the strong aroma of black tea. This Chinese tea undergoes a unique process, including withering the tea leaves under the strong sun and oxidising them before curling and twisting. Best enjoyed without milk, may be sweetened.

Chai Tea
A spiced black tea, cardamom, cinnamon, and ginger. Enjoyed with or without milk.

When the tea menu was written, I knew the varieties and types that I wanted to offer; job done! You would be very much mistaken if that were the case, as I now needed to find out where these teas are from and how they were made. What I am talking about here is the ethical nature of the way tea is produced, harvested, and processed. In one of my earlier chapters, I shared my findings about the chocolate producers who built their empires on unethical cocoa trading. For my teas, I needed more information than just going to the shop to buy the first tea on the shelf. There are some indicators that can help you decide to buy good tea where workers are earning a fair wage and where working conditions, and general support are good. Fairtrade, buying organic, plastic-free, and using loose tea rather than tea bags can all help. It is still difficult to be sure, and, in my opinion, more needs to be done to help the consumer make the best choices when buying tea. For myself, I decided to buy my tea from reputable tea merchants, as they provide the most information to help me choose the teas I want to serve.

After all that talk of tea, it reminded me of my recipe for toasted teacakes. These fluffy pillow-like buns are stuffed with jewels of raisins, orange, and lemon peel, spiced with cinnamon and brown sugar, all contributing to a very seductive aroma when toasted. I make mine for the Story Garden café with vegan butter and soy milk so that my vegan customers are not missing out.

The origin of the tea cakes can be confusing, as it depends on which type you are referring to. Let's start with mine, the dough like ones. I believe that these sweet buns were parts of the 1840s afternoon tea revolution. Over time, various part of the UK came up with their own interpretation. In the north of the UK, in places such as Yorkshire, East Lancashire, and Cumbria, the teacake is a plain roll used to make sandwiches. In Kent, also known as the 'Garden of England', they are called Huffkins, a white bread roll proved over a lengthy time often decorated with a cherry and dimple in the centre to represent a baker's thumb. Nowadays, you will find Huffkins stuffed with bacon and sausages sold all over Kent. The Lady Arundel's Manchet teacake is baked in Sussex and includes cinnamon and nutmeg, as well as the distinctive diamond pattern on the top. The confusion about the tea cakes, among others, is linked to Scotland. In 1956, Scottish bakers baked a small round biscuit and topped it with marshmallow before dipping it into melted chocolate and calling it teacake, also known as Tunnock's teacake. I call mine toasted teacake, so hopefully it will make it clear which one I am talking about. We believe that the Romans were the first people to toast bread in order to extend its shelf life. The word toast is derived from the Latin word "tostus," meaning scorched, roasted or to dry out. In the 19th century, Mrs. Beeton explained in her "Book of Household Management" how to make toast on an open fire without burning the bread. I use a toaster for my vegan teacakes and offer lashings of butter that seep into the crunchy surface before loading it with a dollop of jam.

Vegan Tea Cake Page 148

My vegan teacakes will also go down well with my own version of Aztec-style hot chocolate, which I shared with you earlier. More recently, I have been offering Jamaican cocoa tea, a blend of 100% cocoa, coconut milk, and spices, including the must-have bay leaves. Similar to hot chocolate, cocoa tea is more intense in flavour and much thinner in texture.

Cocoa Tea Page 149

In order to elevate the whole pop-up experience, I started to offer afternoon tea-only events, as it can be easier to calculate costs but is by no means less time-consuming. At the beginning of every afternoon tea, guests are greeted with a welcome drink, which varies depending on the season. My two favourites are homemade ginger beer and sorrel syrup iced water.

Ginger beer, a carbonated ginger-flavoured and sugary drink, became popular in England during the early years of the 18th century, but by the late 18th century, the beer found firm footing in Jamaica, where, to this day, it is a favourite drink. There is an alcoholic version of ginger beer available, but these are labelled 'alcoholic ginger beer,' suggesting all others are alcohol-free. Made from ginger, brown sugar, water, lime, and other recipes available, it is a delicious refreshing drink if served with ice.

The Jamaican Story Garden Ginger Beer Welcome Drink Page 149

The other spiced drink that I offer is sorrel syrup water, which is made from dried hibiscus.

Not to be confused with the sorrel herb, hibiscus syrup is generally enjoyed in the Caribbean and Africa during the Christmas season and can be consumed hot or cold. The hibiscus plants made their way to the Caribbean from Africa with the transport of slaves across the Atlantic. Apart from taking many plants and seeds across the ocean, the hibiscus plants were also used to keep the livestock alive and given to both slaves and animals as a kind of nourishing and medicinal remedy during the long voyages. Later on, these dried hibiscus flowers were soaked in water, spiced with pimento, cinnamon, and ginger, and sweetened with sugar. The syrup is often used to make wines, mixed with rum and, in my case, sparkling water, lime, and ice.

The Jamaican Story Garden Sorrel Syrup Welcome Drink Page 149

It seems ironic to come to the end of my diary and make the last two recipes welcome drinks, but it is meant as a welcome to try all or as many of the delicious recipes that I have featured in this diary. Try them out, make them your own, and without knowing it, you have created your own journey.

For myself, I have come a long way from the little hospital in Schleiden, Germany, where I was born in March 1970. I feel privileged that I have been able to note down some of my most memorable adventures, and I am proud that baking has provided me with an anchor, and it will hopefully do the same for you.

The End
(for now)

The last thing my grandmother told me was:
"In the end, all will be well; if it is not, it is not the end."

I believe that:
"Pastry cooking comes from the heart and the fingertips."

Happy Baking
Yours Andreas

Appreciation

I find it important to take a moment and think about the people who have shown me the way, guided me and inspired me to become the person I am today. We all have memories of individuals who, consciously or unconsciously played a part in our journey. They have influenced us in our decision-making, the good and the not-so-good ones. For myself, I have been inspired by so many, some of whom are personal to me. This last chapter I dedicate to the ones that have, in my opinion, shaped the pastry world, and without them, we would not have this wonderful profession. But it is also a thank you to all of you educators, teachers, and pastry mentors out there, from your mum who taught you how to bake biscuits to the celebrity chefs who motivated you and everyone else in between who has an appreciation for patisserie and confectionery.

My Grandmother

Born Helene Mauel on the 21st of February in 1912 as the oldest of nine children, she was inevitably marked out to become a good cook and baker. She became a widow during WWII when her husband, Matthias Josef Hein, was killed, leaving behind not only his wife but also a daughter and a son, my father. He also left her with his surname, Hein, and when she married again in the 1950s, my dad kept his surname and passed it on to me. She became my inspiration and mentor from the day I was born until her death in 1983. Thank you for introducing me to your bakehouse in the early 1970s and guiding me towards the person I am today.

Marie Antoine Carême

An influential French chef born in the late 18th century who started his culinary journey very much like most hospitality workers by working in basic restaurants, washing up, peeling vegetables, and generally doing all the jobs no one wants to do. In 1798, however, he started an apprenticeship as a pastry chef in Paris, and here he perfected the art of laminating dough and pastry. His strong interest in architecture also led to his elaborate sugar sculptures. After qualifying as a pastry chef, he continued his culinary journey by learning all aspects of cooking. Very quickly, his talents were recognised, and soon, he was creating dishes for royalty and alike. He shared his passion for the industry in many of his books and carried on inspiring so many others right to this day, including myself. He sadly died in his late forties, just before the completion of his five-part book. "The Art of French Cookery". Thanks to his protégée, Armand Plumerey, who completed the last two volumes of his work, Carême's extensive work was completed and is still in circulation today.

George August Escoffier

Also known as the godfather of the culinary world, he spent most of his professional life updating classic French cuisine in the late 19th and early 20th centuries. He based his modernisation on Carême's work in cookery, but he also brought order and discipline into the professional kitchen with the introduction of the staff hierarchical order, which some believe is based on his military background. He is famously associated with running the kitchens at the Savoy and Ritz Hotel in London and had published many books before he died in 1935 at age 88.

Paul Bocuse

A French chef born in 1926 made his mark on the culinary world in the mid-20th century by bringing a lighter touch to French cookery, which became known as nouvelle cuisine. This new way of cooking was brought to the masses in the 1960s and 1970s, where emphasis was placed on freshness, lightness, and clarity of flavour in stark contrast to the more calorific dishes popular until then. This new wave was further influenced by the Japanese way of preparing food. He passed away in 2018, aged 91, leaving behind a huge legacy of chefs who trained under him and numerous publications of his gastronomic delights as well as his passion and enthusiasm for the profession.

Isabella Beeton

Better known as Mrs. Beeton was an English journalist, editor, and writer in the mid- to late- 19th century. Trained in London and Germany, she went on and married her publishing husband, Samuel Orchart Beeton. She is well known for her publications on domestic house management and the "Dictionary of Every Day Cookery." I find her inspirational because she brought confidence in cooking to everyday kitchens, highlighting the fact that you don't have to be as trained as a chef to create something really magical with simple ingredients if you have the passion and determination to do so. Unfortunately, she died in 1865 at age of just 28, but despite her early demise, she became known by many and is still remembered today.

Gaston Lenôtre

Born in 1920, he dedicated his life to patisserie and confectionery right up to his death in 2009. He is widely known for being the creator of the famous opera cake, an almond sponge layered with coffee cream soaked in rum before being covered in chocolate. He was part of the wave created by Paul Bocuse, bringing the classic French patisserie into the 20th century with his creations of lightly whipped mousses and reducing the amounts of sugar and flour in the standard recipes. He is my inspiration because, in 1971, he started his own school just outside Paris, where he trained pastry chefs. I particularly like the fact that, as part of his teaching, he included the science part of each ingredient in his delivery, something very close to my heart. He is often compared to Carême, and he believed that all chefs should be trained in patisserie as it is the best way to learn precision and perfectionism. I could not have said it better myself.

Charles Joughin

An unusual choice for my appreciation, maybe not as well-known, but nonetheless an incredible inspiration to me. This British/American chef, born in 1878, not only had a strong passion for baking but was also fascinated with ships and their voyages. In 1912, he became the chief baker of RMS Titanic, overseeing 13 bakers on the luxury ocean liner. He was crucial in leading so many to safety, including his bakers, and despite not making it into a lifeboat himself, he survived this horrible disaster relatively unharmed. Later on, he continued his passion for baking and ships when, during WWI, he joined the Merchant Navy, again surviving the war and the high seas. He died at age 78 in 1956, but his character went on to be betrayed in films such as "A Night to Remember" and "Titanic." He is the perfect example of never giving up on your passion.

I could go on and mention so many others, as the list is endless, but the ones mentioned above are close to my heart and hopefully inspire you to find out a little more about others and/or the stories of some of your favourite pastry dishes. To help you with that journey, I would finish my diary with some personal recommendations of my top ten pastry books from my bookcase, all of which are still inspiring me today.

Recommendations

Number 1 "The Pasty Chef's Companion" by Glenn Rinsky and Laura Halpin Rinsky, which is a comprehensive resource guide for baking and pastry professionals, a kind of pastry dictionary.

Number 2 "Understanding Baking" by Joseph Amendola and Donald Lundberg, explains the science of baking in plain English.

Number 3 "Patisserie" by L J Hanneman, a pastry bible of the basics.

Number 4 "The Roux Brothers on Patisserie", French patisserie at its best.

Number 5 "Patisserie" by William and Suzue Curley, a modern take on the classics.

Number 6 "The Art of Confectionary" by Ewald Notter, all about sugar craft.

Number 7 "The Art of the Chocolatier" by Ewald Notter, the best book on chocolate.

Number 8 "Couture Chocolate" by William Curly" a truly magical book of chocolate recipes.

Number 9 "Advanced Bread and Pastry" by Michel Suas, a very detailed bread and pastry bible.

Number 10 "Professional Patisserie" by Chris Baker, Mick Burke, Neil Rippington, a book all about pastry used in many training establishments today.

You never stop learning!

My first year as lecturer

My time as a medic avoiding national service.

My other Grandmother

First day at school 1976

Denmark 1992

Wedding Cake 2010

The Bakehouse

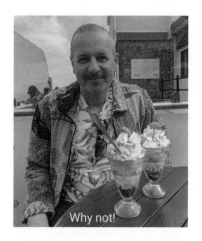

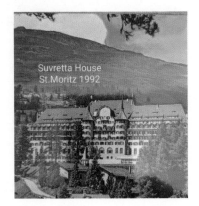

"The Recipe Book"

All recipes have either been passed down to me, reinvented, or modernised over the last 50 years by myself, and I still use them all today.

Baking requirements:

Passion

Love

Patience

A good set of scales

Some basic baking utensils

A good oven

Lots of willing tasters

Baking is a skill, so don't give up if the first batch does not work. Practice makes perfect!

Chapter 1

The early years of growing up and my daily bread

Recipes

1. Zimtsterne

2. Sourdough Bread

3. Brioche

4. Granary Caraway Seed Bread

5. Nussecken

6. Zuckerkuchen

Zimtsterne (Cinnamon Stars)

Make around 30 stars (depending on your cutter size)

350g sieved icing sugar
75g egg whites

125g marzipan
250g ground almonds
8g ground cinnamon

1. Make a royal icing by combining the sieved icing sugar and egg whites using a wooden spoon or a beater if using a machine. It does take a good 5-10 minutes until the icing is thick and glossy, holding shape, but is still soft enough to be spread. Covered up and set aside.
2. Push the marzipan, ground almonds and cinnamon together with a fork or a paddle if using a machine. Once done, add 2/3 of the royal icing to the almond paste and knead until it comes together. Chill for 30 minutes.
3. Roll the chilled biscuit pastry between sheets of greaseproof paper to a medium thickness.
4. Spread the remaining royal icing over the top, allowing the icing to dry and harden up.
5. Once the icing has been set, cut using a star cutter and bake at 160°C for 10 minutes or until light and golden brown.
6. Cool on a cooling rack and store; best eaten after a few days if you can wait that long.

Tips:

- Dip the cutter into warm water before cutting out.
- Alternatively, use a round cutter and cut crescent shapes.
- Left over pastry roll into balls, flatten and press your thumb into the centre. Fill the dimples with jam and bake.

Sourdough

Growing your own starter culture (also known as mother dough)

Day 1:
125g strong white flour
125g rye flour
190ml warm water

1. Mix together in a container with a tight-fitting lid and leave to ferment at room temperature.

Day 2:
125g strong white flour
125g rye flour

190ml warm water

1. Discard ½ of the mix.
2. Add the flour and water to the mix from day 1 and leave to ferment at room temperature.

Day 3:
60g strong white flour
60g rye flour
60ml warm water

1. Discard ½ of the mix.
2. Add the flour and water to the mix from day 2 and leave to ferment at room temperature.

Day 4:
60g strong white flour
60g rye flour
60ml warm water

1. Discard ½ of the mix.
2. Add the flour and water to the mix from day 3 and leave to ferment at room temperature.

Day 5:
60g strong white flour
60g rye flour
60ml warm water

1. Discard ½ of the mix.
2. Add the flour and water to the mix from day 4 and leave to ferment at room temperature.

Day 6:
Make the starter for your first loaf.

250g strong flour
150g mother sourdough starter
275ml warm water

1. Sieve flour and combine with starter and water, cover. The mixture is quite sloppy.

Day 7:
Starter from the night before and add:

300g strong sieved flour
(1/2 teaspoon dried yeast optional only if you are in a rush)
20ml oil
10g salt

1. Combine all the ingredients.
2. Knead to a dough and rest for about 2 hours in a warm place.
3. Knock back, shape and place into an oiled bowl or a proving basket. Prove until double in size; this can take up to 10 hours, faster if you add some dry yeast.
4. Bake on a hot tray dusted with semolina or flour and bake at 240^{0}C for 10 min.
5. Reduce the heat to 200°C and bake until the bread sounds hollow about 20-40 minutes, depending on size.

Tips:

- Make your dough the day before and prove it overnight.
- Once you have made your starter dough, feed it once again as for day 5 and keep it in the fridge.
- If you are not baking every day, keep it in the fridge and feed once a week, keeping it in the fridge after each feed.
- If you are baking a loaf, remove it 2 days before using it from the fridge, feed for one more day and use it again on day 6.
- If you are not making sourdough for a longer period, leave it in the fridge for up to two weeks, feed for two days and then put it back in the fridge for up to two weeks or until required.

Sourdough feed

1. 60g strong white flour
2. 60g rye flour
3. 60ml warm water

Remember to name your sourdough starter; mine is still called Helga, the same as my grandmother called hers.

Brioche

500g strong flour
15g fresh yeast or 8g dry yeast
70ml warm, full-fat milk
4 eggs
15g salt
30g sugar
250g soft butter

1. Sieve flour.
2. Combine yeast and warm milk; be careful not to heat more than 50°C.
3. Beat together the eggs, salt and sugar.
4. Add the yeast and egg mixture to the flour and start kneading.
5. After 5 minutes, knead in the soft butter.

Tips:

- Don't be tempted to use flour when kneading; it will come together.
- Rest in the fridge for at least one hour or overnight.
- Shape to the required size and prove in a warm place until double in size.
- Bake at 180°C until light brown, glaze with egg wash and bake until golden brown.

Granary Caraway Seed Bread

300g strong flour
300g granary or wholemeal flour
10g salt
20g sugar
20g fresh yeast or 10g dried yeast
20g butter
400ml tepid water
10g caraway seeds (optional)

1. Sieve the flours and return the bran and granary seeds back to the flour and mix together with the salt and caraway seeds.
2. Dissolve the yeast in ½ of the tepid water, add the sugar.
3. Allow the yeast water to stand until frothy for about 15 minutes in a warm place.
4. Add the frothy yeast mixture, butter and the other half of the water to the flour and knead for about 10 minutes.
5. Prove until it doubles in size in a warm place.
6. Knock back scale 60g individual rolls or divide the dough into two loaves and shape.
7. Prove until double in size, dust with flour and bake the bread rolls at 210°C until golden brown. The bread loves, bake for 10 minutes at 210°C and then reduce the oven temperature to 180°C for another 20-30 minutes or until the loaves sound hollow when tapped on the bottom.

- Cool on a cooling rack and serve with a lashing of butter, but don't forget the pony!

Nussecken (Nutty Triangles, my mother's recipe)

300g self-rising flour or 300g plain flour and 1 teaspoon of baking powder
130g caster sugar
130g butter
2 eggs
1 teaspoon of vanilla essence
¼ teaspoon of ground cinnamon
150g apricot jam

Filling

200g butter
200g caster sugar
4 tablespoons water
200g ground hazelnuts
200g chopped hazelnuts

Decoration
200g dark chocolate

1. Sieve the flour, add the caster sugar and cinnamon and rub in the cold butter until a bread crumb consistency has been achieved.
2. Add the eggs and vanilla essence and combine all together. Chill for 30 minutes.
3. Roll the sweet pastry base into a 20cm x 30cm Swiss roll tin, pierce all over using a fork and spread a thin layer of apricot jam over the pastry.
4. For the filling, melt the butter, sugar and water and add the nuts.
5. Spread the filling onto the base and bake at 175°C for 20-25 minutes or until golden brown.
6. Allow it to cool before cutting into squares, and then cut each square across to create the triangle.
7. Dip each corner in melted dark chocolate; once the chocolate has set, store in an airtight container for up to two weeks.

Tips:
- You can use almonds or a combination of nuts.
- It's best to temper the chocolate.

Zucker Kuchen (Joy & Sorrow Cake)

300g strong flour
Pinch of salt
40g caster sugar
30g soft butter
1 egg
20g fresh yeast or 10g dried yeast
130ml tepid milk

Method: Sponging method

1. Sieve the flour and salt and place them into a bowl.
2. Dissolve the yeast with the tepid milk and add 1 tablespoon of the sieved flour. Allow it to froth for about 15 minutes in a warm place.
3. Add the frothed yeast to the flour together with the butter, sugar and egg and knead for about 10 minutes into a smooth dough.
4. Rest the dough in a warm place until almost double in size, then knock back and roll into a medium thickness. Place onto a greased tray and push dimples into the rolled-out dough using your fingers.
5. Pipe the butter mixture on top and sprinkle with flaked almonds or crumble.
6. Alternatively, add fruits such as diced apples or plums or any tin fruit onto the butter mixture and cover with crumble.
7. Prove in a warm place for 30 minutes and bake at 180°C for about 20-30 minutes or until golden brown.

Tip:
- Use a deep tray, as the butter can otherwise run out during baking.

Butter Topping

125g butter
250g caster sugar
100g flaked almonds

1. Beat the butter and sugar until light and fluffy; pipe or spoon in small lumps onto the rolled dough and sprinkle with flaked almonds.

Crumble

60g cold butter
60g caster sugar
125g self-rising flour
1 egg yolk

1. Sieve flour and combine it with the sugar.
2. Rub in the cold butter.
3. Gently rub in 1 egg yolk, being careful not to overwork the crumble.

Alternatively, replace the butter topping with custard.

Custard

½ litre milk
45g custard powder
60g sugar
1 teaspoon of vanilla essence

1. Dilute the custard powder with some of the cold milk, add the sugar.
2. Boil the remaining milk with the vanilla essence.
3. Wisk the custard powder into the boiling milk, bubble up and pour into a clean bowl.
4. Cover directly with cling film.
5. Spread the cooled custard over the rolled-out dough.

Chapter 2

Training, military and chocolates

Recipes

1. Vanilla Ice Cream

2. Semolina Pudding

3. Peppermint Granita

4. Pumpernickel Cream

5. German Apple Pie

6. Rote Gruetze

7. House Gateau

8. Prince Regent Cake

9. Rice Pudding

Ice Cream

7 egg yolks
200g caster sugar
500ml double cream
250ml full-fat milk
1 vanilla pod

1. Combine the egg yolks with the sugar and set aside.
2. Scrape the vanilla seeds out of the vanilla pod by cutting the pod in half lengthways.
3. Place both the vanilla seeds and the vanilla skin in a medium-sized pan with the cream and the milk.
4. Heat up just below boiling, and then pour the cream mixture onto the egg mixture, whisk together well and return to the heat.
5. Stir gently, using a wooden spoon, until the mixture reaches 84°C or the back of the spoon is coated.
6. Do not boil the mixture, as it will scramble.
7. Once heated correctly, strain through a sieve and cool down before churning in an ice cream maker.

Add the below to the vanilla ice cream once it has been strained but before it has cooled down.

Chocolate ice cream: add 100g dark, milk, white or ruby chocolate
Hazelnut ice cream: add 100g hazelnut spread
Peanut butter ice cream: add 100g of smooth peanut butter

Semolina Pudding

500ml full-fat milk
1 vanilla pod
Zest of 1 lemon
50g semolina
8 leaves of gelatine
5 egg yolks
125g caster sugar

375ml double cream
40g icing sugar

1. Soak the gelatine in cold water.
2. Whisk up the sugar and egg yolks.
3. Warm the milk, vanilla seeds and lemon zest.
4. Slowly whisk in semolina and keep whisking until it thickens up.
5. Remove from the heat and add the soaked gelatine.
6. Fold in the whisked egg yolks and sugar and allow to cool by whisking over ice.
7. Whip the cream with the icing sugar and fold under the cooled semolina pudding.
8. Pour into the individual mould a large flan mould, individual glasses or cups and set fully in the fridge.
9. Serve with a raspberry coulis.

Raspberry Coulis

300g legally obtained raspberries
150g caster sugar
Juice of 1 lemon (use the leftovers from the semolina pudding)

1. Place all in a pan, simmer for 5 minutes and strain.
2. Cool before serving.

Peppermint Granita

60g icing sugar
700ml sparkling wine
Juice of one lemon
1 tablespoon of chopped mint leaves
Peppermint liqueur (optional)

1. Dust a shallow dish or tray with the icing sugar.
2. Combine the sparkling wine, lemon juice and chopped mint and pour onto the icing sugar.
3. Place into the freezer or on an icy, snow-covered rooftop and freeze.
4. Once frozen, scrape with a spoon, place into a glass and serve.
5. Pour a tablespoon of peppermint liquor over the granita; it is not essential, but delicious.

Pumpernickel Cream

125g finely chopped pumpernickel
1 litre full-fat milk
100g caster sugar
40ml Kirschwasser (or any other schnapps)
1 vanilla pod
4 leaves of gelatine
3 egg yolks
1 litre double cream

1. Warm half of the milk with half of the sugar. Do not boil.
2. Pour the warm milk over the bread, add Kirschwasser or any other snaps and set aside.
3. Soak the gelatine in cold water.
4. Whisk together the egg yolks and remaining sugar.
5. Warm up the remaining milk, vanilla seeds and vanilla skin, pour over the egg yolks and return to the pan.
6. Stir gently, using a wooden spoon, until the mixture reaches 84°C or the back of the spoon is coated. Do not boil the mixture, as it will scramble.
7. Remove from the heat and strain into a clean bowl.
8. Add the gelatine and the soaked bread, cool down.
9. Whisk the cream, and just before the bread mix has set, fold in the whipped cream.
10. Place into individual dishes or one large one.
11. Chill for at least two hours before removing from the mould, serve with raspberry coulis.

German Apple Pie (10-inch flan ring)

Sweet Pastry

400g plain flour
200g caster sugar
150g butter
2 eggs
Pinch of salt
Zest of 1 lemon

Filling

1.2 kg peeled, cored and chopped apples
Juice of 1 lemon
50g caster sugar
1 teaspoon of custard powder
1 teaspoon of aniseed or cinnamon
100g sultanas
100ml apple juice
1 egg

Pastry

1. Sieve the flour and add the sugar, salt and lemon zest.
2. Rub in the cold butter until a breadcrumb texture has been achieved.
3. Add the eggs and combine. Chill for 1 hour.

Filling

1. Add the apples, sultanas, spices, custard powder and sugar into a large pan.
2. Add the lemon juice and apple juice and combine.
3. Heat gently and cook for about 10-15 minutes or until the apples are soft.
4. Allow to cool.

Assembly

1. Divide the pastry into three parts, roll out a base, use one-third for the side and keep one-third for the top.
2. Once the base and sides have been placed into the flan ring, add the cooled-down apple and place the rolled-out pastry lid on top.
3. Brush with beaten egg and bake at 180°C for about 40-50 minutes.
4. Allow to cool before removing the flan ring and serve with whipped cream.

Rote Gruetze & Vanilla Sauce

750g mixed frozen berries
750ml red fruit juice, grape or cherry, alternatively apple juice or red wine
120g sugar
60g cornflour
400g mixed fresh berries (strawberries, raspberries, blueberries)

1. Place the frozen berries and 700ml of the liquid and the sugar into a large pan and simmer for about 10-15 minutes.
2. Strain the cooked berries through a sieve and return the smooth liquid back to the boil.
3. Combine the cornflour and 50ml of the remaining juice together and whisk into the boiling fruit puree. Allow to boil for about 2 minutes.
4. Cool slightly before stirring in the fresh berries.
5. Serve with vanilla sauce.

Vanilla Sauce (Sauce Anglaise - English Cream)

200ml full-fat milk
75ml double cream
1 vanilla pod
1 egg
1 egg yolk
65g caster sugar

1. Boil the milk and the cream with the vanilla seeds and vanilla skins.
2. Whisk together the egg, egg yolk and sugar.
3. Pour the boiling liquid into the eggs and whisk well.
4. Clean out the saucepan and get a clean bowl and a strainer.
5. Return the egg milk to the heat in the clean saucepan and stir gently with a wooden spoon until the sauce starts to thicken.
   Important: DO NOT BOIL THE SAUCE.
6. Pour into a clean bowl and chill.
7. When cold, strain before using.

Almond Rocher

50g granulated sugar
50g water
½ cinnamon stick
250g flaked almonds
250g tempered dark chocolate

1. Boil the sugar, water and cinnamon stick, remove from the heat and infuse the cinnamon for at least 30 minutes.
2. Rub a little stock syrup over flaked almonds and roast in the oven at 175°C until golden brown.
3. Cool almonds, combine with tempered chocolate and spoon into small heaps. Allow to set, decorate as required.

House Gateau (10-inch)

Sweet Pastry Base

30g icing sugar
60g butter
10g egg whites
Pinch of salt
95g plain flour

1. Mix icing sugar, butter, and salt together. Combine, but don't mix it too fluffy.
2. Mix in egg white.
3. Lastly, work in the sieved flour.
4. Be careful not to overwork the sweet pastry.
5. Cool for at least 30 minutes before using.
6. Bake a 10-inch disc at 175°C until golden brown.

Nut Cake

3 eggs
130g caster sugar
1 teaspoon vanilla essence
70g chopped almonds
70g chopped hazelnuts
140g chopped chocolate
50g plain flour
6g baking powder

1. Whisk the eggs. Vanilla and sugar, using an electric mixer, until thick and foamy.
2. Sieve the flour and baking powder and combine with the almonds, nuts, and chocolate.
3. Gently fold the nut mixture into the egg foam, pour into a 10-inch cake tin and bake at 180°C for about 20-25 minutes.

Assembly:

100g melted dark chocolate
50g caster sugar
50g water
10ml rum

1. Spread the melted chocolate onto the baked sweet pastry base and place the nutty sponge on top. Push a 10-inch-tall cake ring around the sponge.
2. Boil the water and sugar, remove from the heat and add the rum.
3. Brush the rum syrup all over the nutty sponge.

Filling Chocolate Chantilly Cream for House Gateau

500ml double cream
50g caster sugar
2 teaspoons of vanilla essence
100g dark chocolate
100ml Advocaat

1. Heat up 100g of the double cream. Once heated, pour over the chocolate and whisk together.
2. Whip up the remaining 400ml double cream, caster sugar and vanilla until half whipped and then whip the cooled-down chocolate cream and whip gently until the filling is holding shape.
3. Spread the chocolate cream over the rum-soaked nutty sponge and once smooth, use the back of a teaspoon and draw 3 circles into the chocolate cream. The cavity created by doing so is then filled with Advocaat. Allow to set for one hour in the fridge.

Finishing

400ml double cream
40g caster sugar
2 teaspoons of vanilla essence
300g grated white chocolate or chocolate curls

1. Whip the cream, sugar and vanilla until almost fully whipped.
2. Remove the cake ring from the gateau and cover the top and sides in the lightly whipped cream.
3. Be careful with the top layer not to smutch the Advocaat.
4. Lastly, cover the cream with the white chocolate and serve.

Prince Regent Cake

190g butter
190g caster sugar
1 teaspoon of vanilla essence
3 eggs
150g plain flour
40g cornflour
3g baking powder
100g melted dark chocolate

1. Cream butter and sugar and vanilla essence.
2. Add eggs slowly.
3. Fold in sieved flour, cornflour and baking powder.
4. Draw 6 times 6-inch circles on trays and divide the mixture into 6 portions. Spread out the mixture and bake at 180°C for about 8-10 minutes or until golden brown.
5. Cool the sponge discs and cut with and 6-inch cake ring.
6. Spread melted dark chocolate onto one of the discs and allow setting in the fridge.
7. Once set, turn it over so that the chocolate side becomes the underside of the cake.
8. Assemble all sponge layers alternatively with chocolate buttercream, finishing with a sponge disc.
9. Allow setting in the fridge and cover in 150g of chocolate ganache.

Chocolate Buttercream Filling for Prince Regent Cake

500ml milk
40g custard powder
10g cocoa powder
200g caster sugar
250g butter

1. Dilute custard powder with some of the cold milk.
2. Bring the remaining milk together with cocoa powder to the boil.
3. Add the milk to the diluted custard powder solution.
4. Return to the heat and boil for 2 minutes.
5. Remove from the heat and stir in the sugar.
6. Place into a bowl, cover with cling film and allow cooling.
7. Cream the butter until light and fluffy, then add cool but not cold custard to the butter until all combined.

Ganache

150ml double cream
1 teaspoon of glucose
150g dark chocolate

1. Chop chocolate, boil cream, glucose and, pour over the chocolate and combine well, cover the cake.

Rice Pudding (4 Portions)

50g pudding rice
50g caster sugar
½ litre milk
10g butter
2-star anis
1 tablespoon of grated fresh ginger
Zest of 1 lemon

1. Warm the milk with star anise, ginger, and lemon zest, remove from the heat and stand for 1 hour. Strain the milk and place it into a clean pan.
2. Wash the rice in cold water.
3. Boil the infused milk and butter.
4. Add the washed rice and stir to the boil.
5. Simmer gently, stirring frequently, until the rice is cooked.
6. Add the sugar.
7. Pour into a pie dish or individual dishes and brown under the grill, or if you have one, use a blowtorch.

Tip:

*   To serve cold, fold in 150g of lightly whipped sugared cream or serve with the "rote gruetze "page 78 .

Chapter 3

Freedom, abroad and finding my feet

Recipes

1. Carrot Cake

2. Engadine Nut Cake

3. Mother Superior's Bircher Muesli

4. Waffles

5. Bienenstich

6. Futjes

7. Danish Pastry

8. Goat Cheese Soufflé

9. Walnut Iced Parfait & Chocolate sauce

10. Black Forest Gateau

Carrot Cake (6-inch cake tin)

100g self-rising flour
20g ground almonds
Pinch of cinnamon
85g caster sugar
85g dark soft brown sugar
2 eggs
120ml vegetable oil
70g grated carrots
40g sultanas

1. Grease and line two 6-inch baking tins.
2. Peel and grate carrots and combine with sultanas, set aside.
3. Sieve flour and cinnamon and add the ground almonds, caster sugar, dark soft brown sugar, eggs and oil and beat all together using a wooden spoon for about 5 minutes.
4. Fold in the carrots and the sultanas.
5. Divide the mixture into two tins.
6. Bake at 180^{0}C for about 25 minutes or until springy to the touch.
7. Cool the cakes.

Topping

250g cream cheese
60ml double cream
50g icing sugar
Juice of ¼ orange

1. Combine all together and lightly beat into a spreadable consistency.
2. Cut each carrot cake in half and spread half the filling in the middle, placing the top half onto the filling.
3. Spread the remaining filling on the top of the carrot cake and cut it into the required size.
4. Decorated with marzipan carrots for that special touch.

Engadine Nut Cake (8-inch)

Sweet Pastry

300g plain flour
100g caster sugar
Pinch of salt
175g butter
1 egg

1. Sieve the flour, add the salt and sugar and rub in the cold butter until a breadcrumb consistency has been achieved.
2. Add the egg and combine the pastry. Chill for 30 minutes.
3. Divide the pastry into three parts; use one part and line an 8-inch cake ring, use another for the sides and use the last third to roll a top lid.

Filling

300g walnuts roughly chopped
200g caster sugar
60g water
200ml double cream
60g honey

1. Combine the sugar and water and bring to a boil until the sugar starts to caramelise.
2. Remove from the heat and add the cream; return to the heat and boil for about 10-15 minutes until thick and creamy.
3. Remove from the heat and add the honey and walnuts; cool the mixture but not too cold.

Assembly

1 egg
Rolled out sweet pastry
Walnut filling

1. Prick the bottom of the rolled-out pastry with a fork.
2. Spread the walnut filing over the pastry.
3. Brush the walnuts with some beaten egg.
4. Place the pastry lid on top and press onto the walnut filling.
5. Use a fork and press down around the edges of the pastry to create a pattern and prick to top again using the fork.
6. Brush with the remaining beaten egg and bake at 175°C for 30-40 minutes or until golden brown.
7. Allow cooling down before serving.

Mother Superior's Bircher Muesli (legally obtained by my mother)

200g oats
100ml water
200ml milk
2 apples grated with skins on
1 medium-sized carrot grated
200g plain yoghurt

1. Soak the oats in water and milk for about 2 hours.
2. Add the grated apples and carrots.
3. Stir in the yoghurt and serve.

My Bircher Muesli Recipe

200g oats
100ml water
200ml oat milk
2 apples grated with skins on
50g sultanas
100g fresh blueberries
1 large tablespoon of honey
200g plain soya yoghurt

1. Soak the oats and sultanas in water and milk for about 2 hours.
2. Add the grated apples, blueberries and honey
3. Stir in the yoghurt and serve.

Waffles

250g butter
200g caster sugar
4 eggs
450g plain flour
30g baking powder
300ml milk
2 teaspoons of vanilla essence
1 tablespoon of rum (optional but utterly delicious)

1. Cream together the butter and sugar until light and fluffy.
2. Combine the eggs with the vanilla and rum and slowly beat them into the butter.
3. Fold in the sieved flour and baking powder as well as the milk.
4. Bake in a preheated waffle maker until golden brown and serve with jam and whipped cream.

Tip:
- Eat the first one for quality control purposes. Grandma is the word…

Bienenstich Kuchen (Bee sting Cake)

Sweet Dough

150ml milk
60g butter
375g strong flour
50g sugar
Pinch of salt
20g fresh yeast or 10g dried yeast

1. Warm the milk to 60°C, remove from the stove and dissolve the butter in warm milk.
2. Add the yeast to the milk and combine with 75g of the sieved strong flour.
3. Let the yeast mixture stand for about 15 minutes.
4. Combine the remaining 300g sieved flour with the salt and sugar and combine with the yeast.
5. Knead into a smooth dough and allow to rest in a warm place, covered up.

Topping

60g butter
50ml double cream
60g caster sugar
20g honey
100g flaked almonds

1. Boil the butter, cream, sugar and honey and reduce for about 2 minutes.
2. Remove from the heat and stir in the flaked almonds.

Assembly

1. Roll out the rested dough into a circle to fit a 10-inch round cake tin.
2. Spread the almond topping over the top and rest for another 30 minutes.
3. Bake at 180°C for about 30 minutes or until golden brown.
4. Once cooled down in the tin, remove from the tin and cut in half horizontal.
5. Cut the top half of the almonds into the required portion size.
6. The bottom half, place into a 10-inch cake ring, and spread the custard filling on top.
7. Place the cut top onto the custard and chill for 1 hour before serving.

Custard Filling

400ml full-fat milk
40g custard powder
1 vanilla pod
1 leave of gelatine
60g caster sugar
250g double cream

1. Soak the gelatine in cold water.
2. Combine the custard powder with 50ml of the milk and the sugar.
3. Boil the remaining milk with the vanilla pod seeds.
4. Pour the diluted custard powder into the boiling milk and boil for about a minute or until it thickens up.
5. Remove from the heat and add the soaked gelatine.
6. Pour the custard onto a shallow tray and cover with clingfilm; allow to cool down.
7. Once cooled down, beat the custard in a bowl until smooth.
8. Whip the cream until almost fully whipped and fold under the cooled and beaten-up custard.

Futjes

190g cream cheese
2 large eggs
75g caster sugar
1 teaspoon vanilla essence
Zest of 1 lemon
190g plain flour
15g baking powder
1 peeled and diced apple (optional)

100g caster sugar
1 teaspoon of ground cinnamon

1. Combine the cream cheese, eggs, vanilla, lemon zest and sugar.
2. Fold in the sieved flour and baking powder.
3. Fold in the apples if using them.
4. Spoon teaspoon size drops into hot oil of 175°C and fry until golden brown.
5. Drain off the oil before coating it in cinnamon sugar.

Tip:

- Replace the apples with nuts or fresh blueberries.

Danish Pastry

340g strong flour
5g salt
60g caster sugar
20g fresh yeast or 10g dried yeast
2 eggs
50ml tepid water
75g tepid milk

1. Sieve flour and combine with salt and sugar.
2. Whisk together the yeast, milk and water, add the eggs.
3. Pour the yeast liquid into the dry ingredients and knead in a dough. Rest in a warm place for about an hour.

175g Butter
30g strong flour

1. Combine the butter with the flour using a fork, and spread onto a piece of greaseproof paper,
2. about 10cm x15cm.
3. Chill for 5 minutes in the fridge.
4. Roll the rested dough into a rectangle around <u>15cm x 20cm</u> and place the prepared butter on top.
5. Fold the long sides of the dough in, covering parts of the butter and the short side, fold over one-third onto the butter. Then, fold the short side over the remaining exposed butter so that no butter is visible or peeking out on the sides.
6. Roll gently into a rectangle 30cm x15cm and fold a third from each side towards the centre dough. Now, you have created three layers.
7. Keep in the fridge for about 30 minutes and repeat twice more, keeping it chilled for 30 minutes after each turn.

Custard Filling

120ml milk
30g caster sugar
1 egg yolk
20g sieved plain flour
1 teaspoon of vanilla essence
10g butter

You also need 100g raisins.

1. Whisk together the sugar and the egg yolk.
2. Add the sieved flour and mix into a paste.
3. Boil the milk with the vanilla essence.
4. Remove the milk from the heat.
5. Whisk in the flour paste.
6. Return to the heat and bring to the boil.
7. Once boiled, remove from the heat and beat in the butter. Pour into a bowl, cover with cling film and chill.

Chocolate Almond Filling

30g butter
30g caster sugar
1 egg yolk (keep the white for the icing at the end)
30g ground almonds
10g cocoa powder
You also need a small tin of apricot halves

1. Cream the butter and the sugar.
2. Slowly add the beaten egg.
3. Sieve the flour and cocoa powder and mix with the almonds.
4. Fold the dry ingredients into the butter mix.

Ready to make custard and raisin roulade

1. Roll half of the dough into a rectangle 30cm x 20cm.
2. Spread the custard over the rolled-out dough and sprinkle with 100g raisins.
3. Roll up the shorter side, and once rolled up, cut into 8 portions.
4. Place onto a baking tray and prove until double in size in a warm place and bake at 180°C until golden brown.

Ready to make chocolate almond and apricot envelopes

1. Roll the remaining half of the dough into a square 20cm x 20cm.
2. Cut into four equal squares and spread a thin layer of the chocolate almond filling over each square, leaving a little gap around the edges.
3. Fold to corners into the centre of each square, slightly overlapping and press down where they meet.
4. Spoon a little more of the chocolate almond cream and place an apricot half onto the blob of chocolate paste.
5. Place onto a baking tray and prove until double in size in a warm place and bake at 180°C until golden brown.

Finishing method

Once baked and cooled, finish with brushing all over with apricot glaze and a drizzle of royal icing.

Apricot Glaze

100g apricot jam

1. Combine with a little water and boil.

Royal Icing

100g icing sugar
A few drops of lemon juice
A tiny bit of egg white (use the leftovers from the chocolate filling)

1. Beat to a thick consistency.

Goat Cheese Soufflé Balsamic Cherries (about 6 Souffles)

50g melted butter
50g finely grated parmesan
6 Ramekins (6cm across)

1. Brush the melted butter all around the ramekins by brushing upwards towards the rim.
2. Coat the greased dishes in parmesan and set aside.
3. Place a shallow tray filled with water in the oven at 175°C.

Goat Cheese Soufflé

65g butter
65g plain flour
60ml milk
1 egg white
250g goat cheese curd
¼ teaspoon of finely ground black pepper
4 egg yolks
3 egg whites
Good pinch of salt

1. Combine the butter and flour using a fork.
2. Gently heat the milk, remove from the heat, whisk in butter and flour and mix.
3. Once all combine together, return back to heat and cook the flour out for about 2 minutes by continually whisking.
4. Remove the mixture from the pan into a clean bowl and whisk to cool down a little.
5. Add the 1 egg white quickly, followed by the 4 egg yolks.
6. Fold in the goat cheese and season with the black pepper.
7. Whisk the egg whites with a generous amount of salt until stiff and fold into the goat cheese mix.
8. Fill the ramekins and level with a pallet knife.
9. Bake in the water bath for 20-25 minutes, ensuring not to open the oven door for the first 20 minutes.
10. Serve in or out of the mould with balsamic cherries.

Balsamic Cherries

200g fresh cherries, stone removed and cut in half
40g demerara sugar
15ml balsamic vinegar

1. Coat the cherries in the vinegar and scatter them onto a shallow roasting tray.
2. Sprinkle the sugar over the top and roast in the oven at 150°C for about 60 minutes, stirring them every 20 minutes. These can be made well in advance and stored in a jar.
3. When serving with the souffle, make sure that they are warmed up.
4. Goes well with some freshly baked bread.

Tip

- If using tin cherries, add all into a saucepan and cook down for 20 minutes until sticky and glossy.

Walnut Iced Parfait & Chocolate Sauce

2 eggs
2 egg yolks
200g honey
1 teaspoon vanilla essence
1 ½ leaves of gelatine
Walnut praline
500ml whipped double cream

Walnut Praline

60g butter
120g caster sugar
125g walnuts

1. Roast the walnuts at 175°C in the oven for about 10 minutes.
2. Melted the butter with the sugar, then caramelise until light golden brown; add the roasted walnuts and pour onto an oiled marble slab or some greaseproof paper.
3. Allow cooling and then crush into small pieces.

Parfait

1. Line a large terrine or long rectangle large cake tin or any other container you can find with cling film.
2. Soak the gelatine in cold water.
3. Whisk eggs, egg yolk, vanilla and honey warm over a water bath until double in size.
4. Whisk cold on the machine or with an electric hand mixer until triple in size.
5. Whip double cream until almost fully whipped.
6. Dissolve gelatine with some of the base mix over a gentle heat and then add whisk back into the base mix.
7. Gently fold in the cream, followed by the crushed walnut praline.
8. Pour into the prepared terrine or container and freeze for at least 3 hours.
9. Cut and serve with chocolate sauce.

Chocolate Sauce (water-based)

250ml water
45g cocoa powder
90g caster sugar

12g cornflour
90ml water

Pinch of salt
90g caster sugar
65g dark chocolate

1. Boil the 250ml of the water together with the cocoa powder and 90g of caster sugar.
2. Mix together the cornflour with the 90ml of cold water.
3. Pour the cornflour mix into the boiling water cook out well.
4. Remove from the heat and add the remaining ingredients.
5. Pour into a cold container, cool and strain when cold.

Black Forest Gateau

Chocolate Sponge

5 eggs
125g caster sugar
1 teaspoon of vanilla essence
100g plain flour
25g cocoa powder
60g melted butter

1. Prepare an 8-inch tin with butter and greaseproof paper on the bottom.
2. Set oven to 175°C - 180°C.
3. Melt butter, pour and set aside to cool down.
4. Bring a small pan of water to the boil.
5. Sieve flour and cocoa powder.
6. Whisk eggs, vanilla essence and sugar, remove the boiling water from the stove and place on the table. Sit the egg mixture on top and whisk until the mixture is light and creamy and has doubled in bulk.
7. Remove from the heat and continue whisking until cold, thick and foamy using an electric mixer. This is referred to as the ribbon stage.
8. Fold in gently the sieved dry ingredients using a spatula in about three stages.
9. Lastly, fold in the melted butter.
10. Pour in the tin and bake for about 20-30 minutes or until springy to the touch.

Cherry Compote

400g drained cherries (ideally sour cherries such as Morella)
150ml of the cherry juice
100g sugar
15g custard powder
20ml Kirschwasser

1. Combine 2 tablespoons of the cold cherry juice with the custard powder and sugar.
2. Boil the remaining juice, and once it starts to boil, whisking the diluted custard powder, boil for one minute, remove from the heat and stir in the drained cherries and the Kirschwasser.
3. Set aside to cool down.

Brushing Syrup

75g sugar
75ml water
30ml Kirschwasser

1. Boil water and sugar, remove from the heat and add the Kirschwasser.

Fresh Cream Filling

600ml double cream
80g caster sugar
1 teaspoon of vanilla essence
30ml Kirschwasser

1. Whip all together to a spreading consistency.
2. Once whipped, put some of the cream into a piping back with a large star nozzle.

Assemble

12 glace cherries, 200g grated dark chocolate shaving or curls

1. Cut the sponge into three slices horizontally.
2. Place the bottom slice of the sponge onto a cake board.
3. Brush with syrup.
4. Spread the cooled cherry compote onto the brushed sponge disc.
5. Spread a quarter of the whipped cream onto the cherries.
6. Place the middle layer of the sponge onto the cream.
7. Brush with syrup.
8. Spread another quarter of whipped cream onto the second layer.
9. Place the top layer of the sponge onto the cream but skin side down.
10. Brush with syrup.
11. Cover the top and side of the gateaux with the remaining cream.
12. Mark the gateaux into 12 portions and decorate with 12 cream rosettes piped from the cream in the piping bag before covering the sides and middle of the gateau in dark chocolate shavings.
13. Chill for at least one hour before indulging in it.

Chapter 4

Rule Britannia

Recipes

1. Scones

2. Devil's Food Cake

3. Sacher Tort

4. Fruit Cake

5. Christmas Pudding

6. Gingerbread

7. Focaccia Bread

8. White Bread

9. Crème Catalan

10. Lemon Tart

11. Chocolate Truffle Torte

12. Tiramisu Torte

13. Cinnamon Soufflé

14. Lekach

15. Pastillage

Scones

250g plain flour
14g baking powder
65g butter
40g caster sugar
1 egg
40g dried fruit such as sultanas
80ml milk plus 1 tablespoon of fresh lemon juice
1 egg for egg wash

1. Squeeze lemon juice into the milk and let the milk curdle.
2. Sieve flour and baking powder.
3. Rub flour, baking powder and butter to a fine crumb.
4. Add the dried fruits.
5. Mix together curdled milk, sugar and 1 egg.
6. Add the liquid to the flour using a wooden spoon; once the mixture becomes too firm, use one hand. It is important to combine all the ingredients into a smooth paste, but at the same time, it is important not to overwork the scone mixture.
7. The combined scone mix should be slightly sticky.
8. Rest for 10 minutes covered up.
9. Roll out, cut into required size, and place onto a buttered tray and egg wash the top, and rest for 10 minutes.
10. Bake at 175°C for 8 - 12 minutes.
11. Remove from the baking tray and cool on a cooling rack.

Scones Filling

1. Cut scones in half using a serrated knife.
2. Place on a chopping board with the top the right way up.
3. Spread a thin layer of jam, such as raspberry jam or strawberry jam, onto the bottom part of the scone.

Chantilly Cream

200ml double cream
1 teaspoon of vanilla essence
25g caster sugar

1. Whisk all to a piping consistency.
2. Place the cream into a piping bag using either a large star or plain nozzle.
3. Pipe the cream onto the jam, place the top onto the cream and lightly dust with icing sugar.

Alternatively, serve with clotted cream.

Devil's Food Cake

320ml full-fat milk
100g dark chocolate
170g butter
360g caster sugar
4 eggs
25ml vanilla essence
285g plain flour
3g baking soda
14g baking powder

1. Grease and line a 10-inch baking tin.
2. Heat the milk and, melt the chocolate in the milk, chill the chocolate milk.
3. Cream the butter and the sugar until light and fluffy.
4. Combine the eggs with the vanilla essence and add gradually to the base.
5. Sieve the flour, baking powder and baking soda.
6. Fold in half the chocolate milk into the base mix, followed by half the flour mixture repeat until all is combined.
7. Pour into the prepared tin.
8. Bake at 175°C for about 45 minutes.
9. Check by inserting a skewer into the centre of the cake. If it comes out clean, the cake is ready to take out.
10. Remove from the tin and cool on a cooling rack.

Devil's Food Cake Filling

330ml double cream
265g dark chocolate
 65g hazelnut spread
 30g butter
200ml semi whipped double cream

1. Boil double cream.
2. Mix together chocolate and hazelnut spread.
3. Pour the hot cream on top of the chocolate mix.
4. Whisk together.
5. Add butter.
6. Cool down, and just before setting, add gently semi-whipped cream.

Assemble

1. Cut the cold Devil's food cake into three horizontally.
2. Place the top layer upside down back into the cake tin, which is lined with baking paper.
3. Spread half the filling onto the cake and cover it with the middle layer of the cake.
4. Spread the remaining filling onto the middle layer and cover with the bottom layer upside down.
5. Set in the fridge for 2 hours.
6. Once chilled, turn upside down out of the tin and cover the whole cake in dark chocolate ganache.

Chocolate Ganache for Devil's Food Cake

200g double cream
200g dark chocolate

1. Boil the cream, pour onto the chocolate and stir together using a whisk.

Sacher Torte

6 egg yolks
125g soft butter
65g caster sugar
125g melted dark chocolate
125g self-rising flour
65g caster sugar
6 egg whites

1. Line two 6-inch cake tins.
2. Melt the chocolate gently over a water bath.
3. Cream butter, sugar and vanilla until light and fluffy.
4. Slowly cream in the egg yolks.
5. Whisk in the melted dark chocolate.
6. Make a French meringue with the egg whites and sugar by whisk in the egg whites in a clean bowl with a pinch of salt until double in size. Slowly whisk in the sugar.
7. Fold the meringue into the base mix, followed by the sieved self-rising flour.
8. Pour the mixture into the prepared tins and bake at 180°C for about 20-25 minutes or until springy to the touch.
9. Cool and cut each cake in half.

Assembly

50ml water
50g caster sugar
30ml rum or brandy
200g apricot jam

1. Boil water and sugar, remove from the heat and add the alcohol.
2. Brush each layer with the syrup.
3. Sandwich together with apricot jam, soaking the top sponge last.
4. Glaze in hot apricot jam to seal.
5. Cover in chocolate ganache.
6. Allow the glaze to set, and write "Sacher" on top in melted chocolate.

Apricot Glaze

100g apricot jam

1. Combine with a little water and boil.

Chocolate Ganache

100g double cream
1 teaspoon of glucose
100g dark chocolate

1.   Boil cream and glucose.
2.   Pour over chocolate and stir until smooth.

Fruit Cake

150g butter
125g dark soft brown sugar
175ml red wine

250g raisins
200g currents
125g sultanas
125g mixed peel
75g glace cherries (chopped up)

3 eggs

250g plain flour
1 teaspoon of mixed spice
1 teaspoon of nutmeg
Pinch of salt
½ teaspoon of baking soda

150ml brandy

1.   Melt the butter with red wine and sugar.
2.   Mix together the raisins, currents, sultanas, mixed peel and cherries.
3.   Pour the melted butter, wine and sugar mixture over the fruits.
4.   Stir in the eggs and combine well.
5.   Sieve flour with the salt, baking soda and spices and fold into the base mix.

How to Bake:

1.   Pour into a lined 8-inch cake tin.
2.   Bake at 175°C for 30 minutes.
3.   Reduce the temperature down to 150°C bake for 30 minutes.
4.   Reduce the temperature to 125°C and bake for 30 minutes.
5.   When baked, leave in the tin and soak in 150ml of brandy.

Tip:

- Make a slop paste by taking two tablespoons of the cake mixture and combining it with two tablespoons of warm water. Pour the slop paste over the cake mixture in the tin before baking. This will create a skin on top of the cake, which will prevent the cake from drying out during baking.

Christmas Pudding (4x 500g puddings or 40 individual puddings)

250g plain flour
250g suet (I use vegetable suet)
50g mixed spice
50g ground almonds
200g bread crumbs

1. Rub all the above together.

300g sultanas
300g currents
300g raisins
200g mixed peel
100g prunes
150g tined apples
100g grated carrots
200g dark soft brown sugar

1. Mix all together

1 orange zest and juice
1 lemon zest and juice
3 eggs
300ml litre dark beer
20ml rum
20ml brandy
20ml sherry
50g black treacle

1. Mix all together
2. Stir the dried fruit mixture into the flour mixture.
3. Fold the liquid mixture into the fruit and flour.

Steaming

- 1000g puddings 6 hours
- 500g puddings 4 hours
- Individual puddings 2 Hours

Gingerbread

240g strong flour
8g baking soda
5g ground ginger
5g mixed spice
60g butter
140g golden syrup
1 egg
80g caster sugar
80g dark soft brown sugar

1. Sieve together the flour, soda, ground ginger and mixed spice.
2. Rub the butter into the dry ingredients.
3. Melt golden syrup with the sugars.
4. Mix all into the crumble, and halfway through, add the egg.
5. Combine until a smooth paste is obtained.
6. Refrigerate for at least 2 hours.
7. Roll out in flour and cut to the required shape.
8. Bake a 160°C for about 12-15 minutes or until set.
9. Cool and assemble with royal icing.
10. Decorate as required.

Tips:

- Bake at a low temperature of 160°C to avoid cracks in your gingerbread.
- Leave space between the gingerbread pieces as the baking soda in the gingerbread will spread outwards.

Royal Icing

300g icing sugar
60g egg whites
A few drops of lemon juice

1. Sieve icing sugar.
2. Combine the egg white with half of the icing sugar.
3. Adjust the icing texture with the remaining icing sugar.
4. Add the lemon juice.
5. Beat into piping consistency.

Focaccia Bread

450g strong flour
15g fresh yeast or 8g dried yeast
150ml tepid water
12g salt
140g mashed potato (no salt)
75ml olive oil
1 tablespoon of chopped rosemary
50g olive oil
1 teaspoon of sea salt

1. Sieve the flour.
2. Mixed yeast with ½ of the tepid water, add two tablespoons of the sieved flour, cover and let stand for 20 minutes until frothy.
3. Warm up the potatoes in the microwave, not too hot, just to take the chill out and mix together with the salt, rosemary and oil.
4. Add the frothed yeast, remaining water and potato mix to the flour and knead into a soft dough for about 10 minutes.
5. Place either into a tray or tin and press your fingers into the dough to create indentations.
6. Drizzle some olive oil over the top and sprinkle with coarse sea salt.
7. Prove until double in size and bake at 210^0C for 30-40 minutes.

Tip:

- Makes a great pizza base (but don't tell the Italians)

White Bread (Choux Pastry Based)

70ml milk
25g butter
40g strong flour
1 egg

1. Make a choux pastry by heating the milk and the butter.
2. Once the butter has melted, boil the milk and add the sieved flour.
3. Cook the flour out using a wooden spoon until it all combines into one lump.
4. Tip onto a cold surface and cool slightly by moving the mixture with the wooden spoon.
5. Place into a bowl and beat the egg into it, again using a wooden spoon, set aside.

Bread Dough

375g strong flour
15g fresh yeast or 8g dried yeast
10g salt
125ml tepid water

1. Sieve the flour.
2. Dissolve the yeast in half of the tepid water, add two tablespoons of the flour. Allow the yeast to froth for about 20 minutes.
3. Add the salt to the flour and combine.
4. Add the frothed yeast mixture and choux pastry and knead all into a dough for about 10 minutes.
5. Let prove until double in size on top of the oven.
6. Knock back, scale, shape, prove and cook 210^0C for about 15 minutes; reduce the heat to 180^0C for a further 20-30 minutes, or when tapped at the bottom, it sounds hollow.

Tips:

- Bakes best in a loaf tin.
- Great bread for toast.
- Add herbs and spices or olives and sun-dried tomatoes, and give your imagination free reign.

Crème Catalan (6- 8 portions, works best in flat ceramic dishes)

500ml full-fat milk
Zest of 1 orange
Zest of 1 lemon
½ stick of cinnamon
8 egg yolks
100g sugar
10g cornflour
100g demerara sugar

1. Roast the cinnamon stick in the oven at 150^0C for about 10 minutes.
2. Warm the milk with the lemon zest, orange zest and the broken-up roasted cinnamon stick.
3. Remove from the heat and infuse for about one hour, then strain the milk into a clean pan.
4. Whisk the egg yolks with the cornflour and sugar.
5. Warm the infused milk and pour onto the egg yolk mix.
6. Return to the heat and continually whisk to boil until thickened up, about 3-4 minutes.
7. Pour the thickened milk into flat ceramic dishes and chill for at least 1 hour.
8. Sprinkle with demerara sugar and caramelised with a blow torch or under a grill.

Lemon Tart

125g plain flour
75g butter
30g caster sugar
1 egg yolk
Pinch of Salt
1 egg white

1. Whisk egg yolk with the sugar.
2. Sieve the flour and salt.
3. Rub the butter into the sieved flour.
4. Make a well and add the dissolved sugar and egg yolk.
5. Lightly mix to a smooth paste.
6. Do not overwork.
7. Wrap in cling film, keeping the pastry flat.
8. Cool before using.
9. When cool, line the flan case with the pastry and blind bake at 180°C.
10. Seal the base with the leftover egg white.

Lemon Tart Filling

3 eggs
140g caster sugar
grated zest of 2 lemons
70ml lemon juice (2 lemons)
85ml double cream

1. Whisk the eggs with the caster sugar and strain.
2. Add lemon zest, lemon juice, and the cream. Continue to whisk until all the ingredients are thoroughly combined. Skim any froth from the top.
3. Pour the filling into the prepared tart case and bake at 120°C for about 30 minutes or until fully set.
4. Chill for at least 1 hour before serving.

Tips:

- When lining the pasty into the flan tin, dock with a fork (pierce holes).
- Line with baking parchment or heat-proof clingfilm before adding baking bean.
- Chill before baking to avoid shrinkage.
- After 20 minutes, remove the baking beans and brush with the egg white.
- Return to the oven until golden brown.
- Bush with egg whites again as soon as it comes out of the oven.
- Place the empty blind baked tart case in the oven and then pour the lemon filling in; this will avoid spilling.

Chocolate Truffle Torte

Gluten Free Chocolate Sponge (10-inch cake tin)

50g gluten-free self-rising flour
½ teaspoon baking powder
20g cocoa powder
30g dark chocolate
100g butter
130g caster sugar
10ml vanilla essence
3 eggs

30g cocoa powder

1. Sieve, gluten-free flour, cocoa powder and baking powder.
2. Gently melt dark chocolate over a water bath.
3. Cream butter, vanilla and sugar until light and fluffy.
4. Gradually add the beaten eggs.
5. Add the melted chocolate.
6. Gently fold in the sieved ingredients.
7. Place into a greased and lined tin and bake at 175^0C for about 20 minutes.
8. Once cooled down, place into a 10-inch cake ring and pour the chocolate truffle filling on top. Set for 2 hours before removing the ring and dust with 30g cocoa powder.

Chocolate Truffle Filling

50ml water
50g caster sugar
50g glucose
2 leaves of gelatine
300g dark chocolate
200ml semi whipped cream

1. Soak the gelatine in cold water.
2. Boil water, sugar and glucose.
3. Remove from the heat and add gelatine.
4. Add melted chocolate and let cool.
5. Semi-whip double cream.
6. Just before setting, fold in the cream.

Tip:

*   Works well with milk white or ruby chocolate as well.

Tiramisu Torte Sponge (8-inches)

75g plain flour
75g caster sugar
½ teaspoon of vanilla essence
3 eggs
20g butter

1. Prepare tin with butter and greaseproof paper on the bottom.
2. Set oven to 175°C–180°C.
3. Melt butter and set aside to cool down.
4. Boil water in a small saucepan.
5. Sieve flour.
6. Whisk eggs, vanilla essence and sugar, remove the boiling water from the stove and place on the table; sit the egg mixture on top and whisk until the mixture is light and creamy and has doubled in bulk.
7. Remove from the heat and continue whisking until cold, thick and foamy using an electric mixer. This is referred to as the ribbon stage.
8. Fold in gently the sieved dry ingredients using a spatula in about three stages.
9. Lastly, fold in the melted butter.
10. Pour in the tin and bake for about 20-30 minutes or until springy to the touch.
11. When cold, cut in half.

Filling

3 egg yolks
150g caster sugar
3 leaves gelatine
600g mascarpone cheese
200ml double cream

1. Soak the gelatine in cold water.
2. Beat the mascarpone until smooth.
3. Semi-whip the cream.
4. Whisk the egg yolks and the sugar warm over a water bath until double in size, remove from the heat and whisk cold using an electric mixer.
5. Place the soaked gelatine into a saucepan and melt with two tablespoons of the cold sabajon.
6. Whisked the dissolved gelatine into the cold sabajon and folded in the mascarpone cheese.
7. Lastly, fold in the whipped cream.

Tip:
- The egg foam is known as sabajon.

Amaretto Coffee Syrup

100ml water
60g sugar
1 teaspoon of instant coffee
20ml amaretto

1. Boil, water, sugar and coffee, and add the amaretto.

50g cocoa powder

Assembly

1. Cut the cooled-down sponge in half and place the bottom of an 8-inch cake ring.
2. Soak the sponge with half of the coffee syrup.
3. Spread half of the filling onto the soaked sponge.
4. Place the top half onto the filling and soak with the remaining syrup.
5. Top with the other half of the filling and chill for 2 hours.
6. Remove from the ring and dust generously with 50g cocoa powder.

Cinnamon Pudding Soufflé (4 Portions based on ramekins size 6cm across by 5cm deep)

20g melted butter
100g caster sugar

1. Prepare 4 ramekins by brushing them out with melted butter and then coat them in caster sugar. Ensure that the rim of the ramekin is also covered.
2. Place a deep tray with water in the oven at 200^0C.

Soufflé

125ml full-fat milk
Good pinch of ground cinnamon
25g soft butter
25g plain flour
2 egg yolks
2 egg whites
35g caster sugar
Pinch of salt

1. Combine the flour with the soft butter into a paste using a fork.
2. Bring milk and cinnamon to the boil.
3. Whisk the flour-butter paste bit by bit into the boiling milk until a thick paste has been obtained; cook out the flour for about 2 minutes.
4. Remove from the pan into a cold bowl and, one by one, whisk in the egg yolks.
5. Whisk the egg white with a pinch of salt until almost fully whisked, then bit by bit, add the sugar until a stiff meringue has been achieved.
6. Gently fold the meringue under the base mix using a spatula.
7. Fill the mixture into the prepared mould almost to the top.
8. Place in the prepared bain-marie and cook for 25-30 minutes.
9. Remove from the oven, dust with icing sugar and serve immediately.

Flavour Variations

- Vanilla Raspberry - place three fresh raspberries in the bottom of the ramekin before filling.
- Chocolate - add 20g of dark chocolate to the milk.

Serve with vanilla sauce, recipe page 78

Lekach

175g golden syrup
50g runny honey
50g dark soft brown sugar
100ml vegetable oil
150ml strong black tea
225g plain flour
1 teaspoon of baking powder
3 eggs
1 teaspoon of ground ginger
1 teaspoon of ground cinnamon
½ teaspoon of mixed spice
50g heated-up honey

1. Grease and line an 8-inch baking tin with parchment paper.
2. Heat up the golden syrup, honey, oil and sugar until the sugar has dissolved.
3. Cool the mixture down before adding the tea and eggs, and beat together well.
4. Sieve all the dry ingredients and fold them under the liquid base mix.
5. Pour into the prepared tin and bake at 160^0C for about 30-40 minutes or springy to the touch.
6. Remove from the oven and brush with the heated-up honey, allowing it to cool in the tin.
7. Cut into the required size.
8. Best made the day beforehand.

Pastillage (suitable for making shapes and bending)

5g gelatine leaves
35g water
280g icing sugar
50g cornflour

1. Soak the gelatine in cold water for 5 minutes.
2. Sieve icing sugar and cornflour.
3. Melt the gelatine and water.
4. Add to the sieved dry ingredients and combine until it all comes together.
5. Place onto a work surface and start kneading until smooth.
6. Use immediately, and store any unused Pastillage in a plastic bag with the air expelled.

Tips:
- A tiny bit of blue food colouring will enhance the whiteness of the Pastillage. If the Pastillage starts to crumble, add a little bit of white fat.
- Roll Pastillage in cornflour and turn during drying
- Colour and be added at the beginning or the end of making Pastillage.

Chapter 5

Education and trips abroad

Recipes

1. Champagne Jelly Panna Cotta

2. Caramel

3. Bun Dough

4. Banana Cake

5. Potato Pasties

6. Quiche

7. Victoria Sandwich

8. Truffles

9. Choux Pastry

10. Croissants

11. Baguette

Champagne Raspberry Jelly & Rosewater Panna Cotta (makes 8 champagne flutes)

Panna Cotta

375ml double cream
125ml milk
¼ teaspoon of rosewater
1 vanilla pod
2 leaves of gelatine
60g caster sugar

1. Soak the gelatine in cold water.
2. Boil cream together with the milk and the vanilla pod seeds.
3. Pour boiling liquid through a sieve onto the sugar.
4. Add gelatine, rosewater and whisk all together.
5. Cool over ice, stirring occasionally, and fill into champagne flutes just before it starts setting.

Champagne Jelly

150ml cranberry juice
30g caster sugar
250ml pink sparkling wine (alcohol or not)
2 leaves of gelatine
125g fresh raspberries

1. Boil juice and sugar for about 5 minutes.
2. Soak the gelatine in the sparkling wine.
3. Remove the soaked gelatine from the sparkling wine and add the hot juice
4. Cool the juice for 30 minutes, pour in the sparkling wine and gently pour onto the set panna cotta.
5. Place in the fridge and add 3-4 raspberries to each jelly.
6. Chill for 2 hours before serving.

Caramel

Dry Caramel

400g caster sugar
Juice of 1 lemon
200ml water

1. Boil water.
2. Use another clean pan and heat up.
3. When the empty pan gets hot, sprinkle the caster sugar in stages in the pan, and every time it starts to brown, add more sugar using a wooden spoon.
4. Once all the sugar has melted and is golden brown, remove it from the heat and add the lemon juice; carefully, it will splash.
5. Slowly add the boiling water and boil all for about 5 minutes or until thick and glossy.
6. Use as required.

Wet Caramel

100g granulated sugar
1 teaspoon of glucose
40ml water

1. Combine all in a clean saucepan.
2. Wash down the sides with cold water and boil until golden brown.
3. Do not stir during boiling.
4. When the desired colour has been reached, dip the outside of the hot sugar pan into a bowl of cold water.
5. Use as required.

Bun Dough

4 Chelsea Buns/ 4 Devonshire Spilts

300g strong flour
10g milk powder
Pinch of ground cinnamon
Pinch of salt
40g caster sugar
30g soft butter
1 egg
20g yeast or 10g of dried yeast
130ml tepid water

1. Sieve the flour and place it into a bowl with the cinnamon.
2. Dissolve the yeast with the tepid water and a good pinch of sugar, add two tablespoons of the sieved flour and allow the yeast to froth for about 20 minutes.
3. Add the milk powder and salt to the sieved flour, followed by the frothed yeast, butter, sugar and egg.
4. Once all combined, place onto a lightly floured surface and knead until smooth and free from stickiness.
5. Keep covered and proven, knock back and use as required.

Tip:
- If you don't have milk powder, replace the tepid water with tepid milk.

Chelsea Buns

(when making both, remove 120g of the dough and use the remaining dough.

50g melted butter
50g dark soft brown sugar
½ teaspoon of mixed spice
25g mixed peel
50g currents

1. Roll out the bun dough into a rectangle.
2. Brush with melted butter.
3. Sprinkle with the dark, soft brown sugar and the mixed spice.
4. Sprinkle with currants and mixed peel.
5. Roll up in a Swiss roll fashion.
6. Cut into 2-inch pieces and place into deep buttered moulds or sit onto a tray.
7. Prove until double in size.
8. Bake at 180°C until golden brown.
9. When fully baked, cool on a cooling rack and brush with bun wash.

Bun Wash

100g sugar
125ml water or milk

1. Boil both together until the consistency of thick syrup.
2. Glaze the Chelsea buns with bun wash when still hot.

Devonshire Split
(Swiss bun or iced finger filled with jam & cream. Use the 120g of the reserved dough)

1. Scale the dough into 30g pieces and roll it into finger shape.
2. Place onto a greased baking tray.
3. Prove until double in size.
4. Bake at 180°C until golden brown.
5. Allow it to cool slightly before placing it onto a cooling rack.
6. When cooled down but still warm, glaze with water icing.

Water Icing

200g icing sugar
30ml water

1. Sieve icing sugar.
2. Add water and beat all together using a wooden spoon.
3. Cool the Swiss buns, cut open fill with jam and whipped cream.

Banana Cake (6-inch cake tin)

100g bananas (the older, the better)
100g caster sugar
35g melted butter
35ml olive oil
1 egg
110g self-rising flour
30g chocolate chips
1 teaspoon of ground cinnamon

1. Mash the bananas and whisk together with the sugar and cinnamon.
2. Add the egg.
3. Mix butter and oil together and add to the base mix.
4. Lastly, fold in the sieved flour and chocolate chips.
5. Pour into buttered and floured tin.
6. Cook at 175°C for 15-20 minutes.
7. Decorated with chocolate royal icing.

Chocolate Royal Icing
80g icing sugar
10g cocoa powder
20g egg white
A few drops of lemon juice

1. Sieve icing sugar, cocoa powder and add egg white and lemon juice; beat with a wooden spoon until shiny and glossy.

Short Crust Pastry for Potato Pasties or Quiche

250g plain flour
Pinch of Salt
50g butter (or 100g butter instead of lard)
50g lard or vegetable lard
10g cornflour
100ml cold water

1. Sieve flour, cornflour and salt.
2. Rub in the fat.
3. Add cold water mix, knead and relax in the fridge.

Potato Filling

250g par-cooked potatoes cut into large cubes
½ leek cooked off
1 teaspoon of freshly chopped rosemary
Salt, Pepper
100g grated cheddar

1. Combine all the ingredients.
2. Roll the pastry in 4x 6-inch circles and brush with some egg wash.
3. Dive the potato filling between the four pasties and fold the pastry in half.
4. Press the joints down with a fork to seal, cut a cross into the pastry, brush with more egg wash and bake at 180°C for 20-30 minutes or until golden brown.

Quiche Lorraine

125g chopped ham or bacon
60g grated gruyere cheese
1 egg
75ml milk
75ml double cream
75g sliced onion
Salt and pepper

1. Line an 8-inch pastry case with short-crust pastry, blind bake and seal with egg yolk.
2. Sweat the sliced onion with the ham or bacon in a frying pan for about 5 minutes, cool down, and scatter into the blind-baked pastry case.
3. Beat egg with the salt and the pepper, add the cream and the milk.
4. Pour egg milk into the flan case.
5. Sprinkle grated cheese over the top.
6. Cook at 175°C for about 25 minutes or until set and golden brown.

Victoria Sandwich

100g butter
100g caster sugar
100g plain flour
2 eggs
5g baking powder
1 lemon zest
10g vanilla essence
150g raspberry jam
Chantilly cream
Icing sugar to dust

- Prepare two 6-inch cake tins.
- Butter and flour the tins and then line the bottom of the tin with greaseproof paper.

1. Cream the butter and sugar until soft and fluffy.
2. Beat the eggs with the lemon zest and vanilla essence.
3. Add the eggs gradually to the butter.
4. Sieve the flour and baking powder and fold in gently.
5. Divide into two 6-inch greased sponge tins.
6. Bake at 175°C for about 12-15 minutes.
7. Turn out onto a wire rack to cool.
8. Spread one half with jam.
9. Spread cream onto the top of the jam.
10. Cut the other half into 6 pieces and place them on top of the cream.
11. Lightly dust with icing sugar.

Chantilly Cream Filling

100ml double cream
½ teaspoon of vanilla essence
20g caster sugar

1. Whisk all to a spreading consistency.

Truffles

Dark Chocolate Truffles

115g dark chocolate
150ml double cream

Milk Chocolate Truffles

115g milk chocolate
100ml double cream

White Chocolate Truffles

115g white chocolate
100ml double cream

1. Chop chocolate unless you use the buttons.
2. Boil cream and pour over chocolate and stir together gently.

Process 1:

1. When almost set, beat with a whisk in order to aerate the ganache.
2. Pipe onto greaseproof paper and allow setting before dusting with cocoa powder.

Process 2:

1. Allow to fully set in the fridge, and when cold, spoon small pieces and roll into balls.
2. When fully set, dust into cocoa powder.

Choux Pastry

125 ml/g water
40g butter
80g strong flour
2 eggs
Pinch of caster sugar
Pinch of salt

1. Sieve the flour.
2. Boil the water with the butter, sugar and salt.
3. Add the sieved flour to the boiling water all at once and stir with a wooden spoon until all comes to a mass. Push the mixture against the sides of the pan.
4. Remove from the heat and tip the mixture directly onto the table.
5. Cool for 2-3 minutes, moving the mixture about with the wooden spoon.
6. Place into a bowl.
7. Crack eggs into a bowl and lightly beat using a fork.
8. Add the eggs in several stages to the mix and keep mixing with a wooden spoon until the eggs have fully combined with the mix. Continue until all the eggs have been used up.
9. Pipe into the required shape and bake at 200°C until golden brown.

Choux Pastry can be used for:

- Éclairs
- Profiteroles
- Horseshoes
- Paris Brest (Choux Pastry Ring)
- Swans

Tips:

- Bake choux pastry products between 190^0C - 200^0C.
- The raising agent in choux pastry is mainly water, which turns into steam in the oven, making the choux pastry product rise.
- If that process is interrupted, the choux pastry product will collapse.
- Therefore, it is important not to open the door during the first 12-15 minutes of baking.
- To check if the choux pastry products are fully baked inside, open the oven door, take one out and close the oven door immediately. Break the product open, and it should feel slightly damp but not moist.
- After the choux pastry product has been removed from the oven, cool the products on a cooling rack. If left to cool on the baking tray, the choux pastry products will sweat, making the overall product soggy.

Finishing Methods for Choux Pastry Products

Choux pastry products can be filled with Chantilly cream, fresh fruits and glazed with ganache, melted chocolate or fondant.

Chantilly Cream

Double cream whipped together with caster sugar and vanilla essence. Depending on the amount of cream used, add the sugar and vanilla essence to taste.

Chocolate Ganache

1 part of dark chocolate to 1 part of double cream

1. Chop the chocolate into small pieces and place into a bowl.
2. Boil the cream and pour the boiling cream onto the chocolate.
3. Gently stir together with a whisk.

Melted Chocolate
Melt chopped chocolate over a bain-marie, ensuring that the water does not boil.

Choux Pasty Filling

Hazelnut Custard

225ml milk
60g caster sugar
2 egg yolks
30g sieved plain flour
1 teaspoon of vanilla essence
1 leaf of gelatine
60g hazelnut spread

1. Soak the gelatine in cold water.
2. Whisk together the sugar and the egg yolks.
3. Add the sieved flour and mix into a paste.
4. Boil the milk with the vanilla essence.
5. Remove the milk from the heat.
6. Whisk in the flour paste.
7. Return to the heat and bring to the boil.
8. Once boiled, pour into a bowl and add soaked gelatine and hazelnut spread, cover with cling film and chill.

Finishing Method

Beat the chilled hazelnut custard until smooth, set aside.

300ml double cream
25g caster sugar
1 teaspoon of vanilla essence

1. Whip the cream with the sugar and vanilla essence and fold under the hazelnut custard.
2. Use as required.

Craquelin

50g plain flour
50g caster sugar
40g butter
Food colour

1. Sieve the flour, add the sugar, rub in butter. When it starts to form a paste, add food colour and work into a dough. Roll out between greaseproof paper very thin, chill and cut to the required size.

Tip:
- When using craquelin on choux pastry, bake at 180°C to maintain the colouring.

Croissants

Basic bun dough

340g strong flour
5g salt
70g caster sugar
20g yeast
200ml tepid water

1. Dissolve the yeast in tepid water.
2. Sieve flour, add salt, sugar and diluted yeast.
3. Knead into a smooth dough and rest in the fridge for one hour.

200g butter
35g strong flour

1. Combine the butter with the flour using a fork, and spread onto a piece of greaseproof paper, about 10cm x15cm.
2. Chill for 5 minutes in the fridge.
3. Roll the rested dough into a rectangle around 15cm x 20cm and place the prepared butter on top.
4. Fold the long sides of the dough in, covering parts of the butter and the short side, fold over one-third onto the butter. Then, fold the short side over the remaining exposed butter so that no butter is visible or peeking out on the sides.
5. Roll gently into a rectangle 30cm x15cm and fold a third from each side towards the centre dough. Now, you have created three layers.
6. Keep in the fridge for about 30 minutes and repeat twice more, keeping it chilled for 30 minutes after each turn.
7. To make the croissants roll into a large rectangle approximately 30cm wide by 60cm long.
8. Cut into triangles and roll from the widest point towards the pointed end.
9. Brush with egg wash and proof for 2 hours or in the fridge overnight.
10. Bake at 190°C for 15-20minutes.

Baguette

450g strong flour
15g fresh yeast or 8g dried yeast
300ml tepid water
1 ½ teaspoons of salt
1 teaspoon of sugar

1. Sieve the flour and salt.
2. Dissolve the yeast with warm water, sugar and about 100g of the sieved flour.
3. Allow to stand for 20 minutes.
4. Combine with the remaining sieved flour and knead into a soft dough.
5. Prove for 40 minutes in a warm place, divide into three and roll into long sticks.
6. Brush with water and allow to prove until double in size.
7. Just before baking at 220°C for 10 minutes, slash the top with a sharp knife and brush again with water.

Chapter 6

Commitment and wedding cakes

Recipes

1. Passionfruit Cake

2. White Chocolate Coconut Lime Cake

3. Rothchild's

4. Mint Tiles

5. Aztec Hot Chocolate

6. Chocolate Tempering

7. Rosemary Chocolates

8. Rum Chocolates

9. Tarragon & Mustard Framing Ganache

Passionfruit Cake

320ml full-fat milk
100g dark chocolate
170g butter
360g caster sugar
4 eggs
25ml vanilla essence
285g plain flour
3g baking soda
14g baking powder

1. Grease and line a 10-inch baking tin.
2. Heat the milk and, melt the chocolate in the milk, chill the chocolate milk.
3. Cream the butter and the sugar until light and fluffy.
4. Combine the eggs with the vanilla essence.
5. Add the eggs to the base mix, one at a time.
6. Sieve the flour, baking powder and baking soda.
7. Fold in half the chocolate milk into the base mix, followed by half the flour mixture repeat until all are combined.
8. Pour into the prepared tin.
9. Cook at 175°C for about 45 minutes.
10. Check by inserting a skewer into the centre of the cake. If it comes out clean, the cake is ready to take out.
11. Remove from the tin and cool on a cooling rack.

White Chocolate Passionfruit Filling

40g passionfruit juice
40g caster sugar
40g glucose
2 leave of gelatine
225g melted white chocolate
300ml semi whipped double cream
150g white chocolate shavings

1. Soak the gelatine in cold water.
2. Boil, sugar, glucose and passionfruit juice.
3. Remove from the heat, add gelatine.
4. Add melted chocolate and let cool.
5. Just before setting, fold in the cream.

Passionfruit Syrup

100g passionfruit juice
25g caster sugar

1. Boil passionfruit syrup and sugar.

Assemble

1. Cut the cold chocolate cake into three horizontally.
2. Place the top layer upside down back into the cake tin, which is lined with baking paper.
3. Soak the cake in a third of the passion fruit syrup.
4. Spread half the filling onto the cake and cover it with the middle layer of the cake.
5. Soak with another third of the passionfruit syrup.
6. Spread the remaining filling onto the middle layer and cover with the bottom layer upside down.
7. Soak the top layer with the remaining third of the passionfruit syrup.
8. Set in the fridge for 2 hours.
9. Once chilled, turn it upside down out of the tin and cover the whole cake in dark chocolate ganache, and decorate it with white chocolate shavings.

Chocolate Ganache

200g double cream
200g dark chocolate

1. Boil the cream, pour onto the chocolate, and stir together using a whisk.

White Chocolate Coconut Lime Cake

320ml coconut milk
100g white chocolate
Zest of 2 limes
170g butter
360g caster sugar
4 eggs
25ml vanilla essence
285g plain flour
3g baking soda
14g baking powder
50g desiccated coconut

1. Grease and line a 10-inch baking tin.
2. Heat the coconut milk and, melt the chocolate in the milk, chill the chocolate milk.
3. Cream the butter, lime zest and sugar until light and fluffy.
4. Combine the eggs with the vanilla essence.
5. Add the eggs to the base mix, one at a time.
6. Sieve the flour, baking powder and baking soda and mix with the coconut.
7. Fold in half the chocolate milk into the base mix, followed by half the flour mixture repeat until all is combined.
8. Pour into the prepared tin.
9. Cook at 175^{0}C for about 45 minutes.
10. Check by inserting a skewer into the centre of the cake. If it comes out clean, the cake is ready to take out. Remove from the tin and cool on a cooling rack.

White Chocolate Lime Filling

40g lime juice
40g caster sugar
40g glucose
2 leaves of gelatine
225g melted white chocolate
300ml semi whipped cream
150g white chocolate shavings

1. Soak the gelatine in cold water.
2. Boil, lime juice, sugar and glucose.
3. Remove from the heat, add gelatine.
4. Add melted chocolate and let cool.
5. Just before setting, fold in the cream.

Lime Syrup

100g lime juice
25g caster sugar

1. Boil lime juice and sugar.

Assemble

1. Cut the cold chocolate cake into three horizontally.
2. Place the top layer upside down back into the cake tin, which is lined with baking paper.
3. Soak the cake in a third of the lime syrup.
4. Spread half the filling onto the cake and cover with the middle layer of the cake.
5. Soak with another third of the lime syrup.
6. Spread the remaining filling onto the middle layer and cover with the bottom layer upside down.
7. Soak the top layer with the remaining third of the lime syrup.
8. Set in the fridge for 2 hours.
9. Once chilled, turn upside down out of the tin and, cover the whole cake in white chocolate ganache and decorate with white chocolate shavings.

White Chocolate Ganache

180g double cream
300g half-melted white chocolate

1. Boil the cream and pour onto the half-melted white chocolate, and stir together using a whisk.

Rothschild

125g caster sugar
125 ground almonds
25g strong flour
125g egg whites
25g caster sugar
Pinch of cream of tartar
100g nibbled almonds

1. Sieve caster sugar, almonds and flour.
2. Whisk egg whites cream of tartar with the 25g sugar into a firm méringue.
3. Gradually fold in the dry ingredients and place in to piping bag with a large star nozzle.
4. Pipe into teardrop shapes, sprinkle with nibbled almonds and bake at 175^{0}C for about 20 minutes.
5. Cool and drizzle in 100g tempered dark chocolate.

Mint Tiles

150g dark chocolate
15g cocoa butter
¼ teaspoon of mint essence
20g demerara sugar

1. Melt chocolate and cocoa butter to 45°C and temper to 30°C – 31°C using the ice method.
2. Add the mint essence and sugar.
3. Spread onto acetate, and just before setting, cut to the required size.

Ice Tempering Method: Melt covertures in a water bath to 45°C - 47°C, cool 2/3 over ice until 25°C, remove from the ice, add the warm chocolate and bring to 30°C -31°C.

Aztec Hot Chocolate

500g water
20g cocoa powder
25g light brown sugar (optional)
1 teaspoon of cinnamon
100g dark chocolate 80%

1. Boil water, cocoa powder and sugar for 3 minutes.
2. Add the spices and 100g dark chocolate.
3. Blend in a blender.
4. Serve.

Chocolate Tempering

Tempering is the process by which couverture is made workable so that the end product has:

- A good gloss
- A hard surface
- A good shelf life
- No fat or sugar bloom
- A brittle snap when fractured

Methods of tempering:

a. Slap method:
Melt covertures in a bain marie to 45°C - 47°C, pour 2/3 onto a marble slab, and work the covertures until it begins to thicken using palette knives and a large scraper. Return to the melted coverture, combine and bring to the required temperature.

b. Cooling method: Melt covertures in a bain marie to 45°C -47°C cool over ice until it starts to thicken and bring up to the required temperature. If gone over, you must start again.

c. Seeding method: Melt chocolate to 45°C - 47°C and add small pieces of cold chocolate until it begins to thicken, and then bring to the required temperature.

d. Direct warming: Melt chocolate, but ensure that the chocolate is not warmed higher than the required temperature. Only possible with chocolate that has not been melted before, as newly bought chocolate is already tempered.

Dark chocolate:
- Warm the chocolate slowly to 45°C -47°C cool down to 24°C warm to 30°C -31°C.

Milk chocolate:
- Warm the chocolate slowly to 45°C -47°C cool down to 24°C warm to 29°C -30°C.

White chocolate:
- Warm the chocolate slowly to 45°C -47°C cool down to 24°C warm to 28°C -29°C.

Gold chocolate:
- Warm the chocolate slowly to 45°C -47°C cool down to 24°C warm to 28°C -29°C.

Ruby Chocolate
- Warm the chocolate slowly to 45°C -47°C cool down to 24°C, warm to 29°C -30°C.

Rosemary Chocolates

Chocolate Shell using a 15-piece mould rubber mould.

200g dark chocolate
20g cocoa butter

1. Melt dark chocolate and cocoa butter and temper using the ice method.
2. Make a shell using the rubber mould by pouring the tempered chocolate into the mould right to the top, shake a little and after one minute, turn the mould over, allowing the chocolate to run out of the mould, leaving a thin coating behind.
3. Keep the remaining chocolate in a warm place.
4. Allow to set a little and fill with the ganache.
5. Allow the ganache to set for 5 minutes in the fridge.
6. Spread the remaining chocolate over the ganache to close each chocolate.
7. Scape off the excess chocolate.
8. Allow fully set in the fridge for about an hour, then remove from the mould.

Ganache

60g double cream
½ teaspoon of chopped rosemary
120g milk chocolate

1. Boil cream, add the rosemary and infuse for about 5 minutes.
2. Heat the rosemary-infused cream and strain over the half-melted milk chocolate.
3. Stir together.
4. Cool until piping consistency and pipe into prepared shells.
5. Close the shells with tempered chocolate.

Tips:
- Use the leftover ganache and chocolate to make a hot chocolate.
- Make the ganache first before you make the shells.

White Chocolate Rum Chocolates

Coloured cocoa butter
Melt cocoa butter, and speckle into prepared moulds

200g white chocolate
20g cocoa butter

1. Melt white chocolate and cocoa butter and temper using the slap method.
2. Make a shell using the rubber mould by pouring the tempered chocolate into the mould, right to the top, shake a little and after one minute, turn the mould over, allowing the chocolate to run out of the mould, leaving a thin coating behind.
3. Keep the remaining chocolate in a warm place.
4. Allow to set a little and fill with the ganache.
5. Allow the ganache to set for 5 minutes in the fridge.
6. Spread the remaining chocolate over the ganache to close each chocolate.
7. Scape off the excess chocolate.
8. Allow fully set in the fridge for about an hour, then remove from the mould.

Rum Ganache

55g double cream
120g milk chocolate (or white or dark)
10g rum

1. Half melt the chocolate.
2. Boil cream.
3. Add the hot cream to the chocolate.
4. Stir together and add alcohol.
5. Cool until piping consistency and pipe into shells.

Tip:

- Make the filling first before making the shells

Tarragon Mustard Framing Ganache

(you need a 4-inch square frame with you can make from thick card or use a shallow tray)

Chocolate Cocoa Butter Solution

10g cocoa butter
20g dark chocolate

1. Melt both to 45^{0}C.
2. Cool slightly before brushing onto acetate for framing the ganache.
3. Pour ganache on top to cocoa brushed acetate and allow to firm up before brushing with more cocoa butter solution on the top.
4. Allow to fully firm up in the fridge.
5. Cut to the required size, dip in dark-tempered chocolate, and set on either a plain, printed or embossed acetate sheet.

Tarragon Mustard Ganach

50ml double cream
125g dark chocolate half-melted
½ teaspoon of mustard powder
½ teaspoon of fresh tarragon
15g butter

1. Boil cream, mustard powder and tarragon.
2. Infuse for 5min, reheat again and strain over half melted chocolate.
3. Stir together with the butter.
4. Pour into a small frame tin lined with acetate or cling film.
5. Allow setting in the fridge for about 30 minutes.
6. Cut to the required size or 16 pieces.

Milk Chocolate Tempering

200g milk chocolate
20g cocoa butter

1. Temper using the slap method.
2. Dip cut framing ganache into tempered chocolate and set onto a printed transfer sheet or textured plastic impression sheet.

Chapter 7

Competitions, adventure and technology

Recipes

1. Khanom Kleep Lamduan

2. Woodapple Doughnuts

3. Vanilla Coconut Panna Cotta & Coconut Tiles

4. Ambassador Cake

5. Lemon Posset & Shortbread

6. Swiss Roll

7. Chocolate Fondant

8. Macaron

9. Welsh Cakes

10. Parkin

11. Battenberg

Khanom Kleep Lamduan

70g plain flour
60g icing sugar
3-4 tablespoons of vegetable oil
1 Thai scented candle

1. Sieve the flour and icing sugar three times.
2. Slowly work in the oil using a fork with the aim of binding the dry ingredients together so that they just hold.
3. Rest for 20 minutes at room temperature.
4. Divide the pastry into 15 pieces, rolling each piece into a ball.
5. Quarter each ball and push three quarters together at the bottom, creating a three-petal flower shape.
6. Use the remaining quarter, roll into a ball and place into the centre of each flower.
7. Bake at 150^{0}C for about 12 minutes so that the biscuits are set but do not colour.
8. Cool the biscuits and place in a container with a lid.
9. Light the Thai candle on both sides, blow out and place in the box with the biscuits, closing the lid tightly, for about 30 minutes.

Tip:
*   You can flavour the pastry with vanilla or rosewater if you don't have the Thai candle, or if you have, do both.

Wood Apple Doughnuts

85g cream cheese
Pinch of salt
1 egg
35g caster sugar
1 lime zest
1 teaspoon of tamarind paste

85g self-rising flour
50g finely diced cooking apple
100g woodapple jam (or Quince jam)
50g sugar with a good pinch of salt and ground cinnamon

1. Peel and dice the apple.
2. Combine the cream cheese, salt with the eggs, lime zest, sugar and tamarind paste.
3. Sieve the flour and add to the mix with the diced apples.
4. Pipe into doughnut moulds and bake at 160^{0}C for 4 minutes until set but no colour. Cool and fry in hot fat at 180^{0}C until golden brown.
5. Drain off the fat and, toss in cinnamon salted sugar and fill with the woodapple jam.

Vanilla Coconut Panna Cotta (12 small wine glasses)

375ml double cream
125ml coconut milk
1 vanilla pod
2 leaves of gelatine
60g caster sugar
1 freshly coconut grated

1. Soak the gelatine in cold water.
2. Boil cream, coconut milk and vanilla pod seeds.
3. Pour boiling liquid through a sieve onto the sugar.
4. Add gelatine and whisk all together.
5. Cool over ice, stirring occasionally, and fill into glasses just before it starts to set.
6. Top with grated coconut.

Tips:
- Cool over the ice as the vanilla seeds are heavy, and when filled into the glasses too early, they will sink to the bottom of the glass.
- I also serve with finely cut pineapple.

Coconut Tiles

50g desiccated coconut
50g icing sugar
10g plain flour
35g melted butter
35g egg whites

1. Melt the butter.
2. Sieve the flour and icing sugar and mix together with the coconut.
3. Add the cool melted butter and the egg white.
4. Rest in the fridge for ½ hour before using.
5. Dip your palette knife into a jug of warm water and spread the mixture onto a baking sheet lined with a splat mat.
6. Bake at 175^0C until they start to brown; remove from the oven, cool and bake again until golden brown. By baking them twice, a more even colour is achieved.

Ambassador Cake

125g dark chocolate
100g butter
75g icing sugar
2 egg yolks
2 egg whites
25g caster sugar
60ml double cream
100g shortbread biscuits
40ml Kirsch or Rum
40g glace cherries chopped

1. Crush the shortbread and mix with chopped cherries and Kirsch.
2. Melt the chocolate and butter over a water bath and once melted, beat in the egg yolks and icing sugar.
3. Semi-whip the cream and fold in.
4. Whisk the egg whites with a pinch of salt until stiff. Slowly whisk in the caster sugar.
5. Fold the meringue into the chocolate mixture, followed by the soaked biscuits.
6. Fill into clingfilm-lined moulds and set in the fridge for at least 2 hours before removing from the mould and decorating with whipped cream.

Tips:
- Make them individually by lining coffee cups with cling film.
- Use the Chantilly cream recipe on page 114 to decorate.

Lemon Posset

100ml lemon juice (2 lemons)
Zest of one lemon
125g caster sugar
425ml double cream
Pinch of nutmeg
Pinch of ground ginger
20g of toasted flaked almonds
20g mixed peel

1. Dissolve the sugar in the lemon juice with zest in a pan over a low heat set aside.
2. Gently heat the cream with the spices, bring to a boil and pour over the lemon syrup.
3. Sieve the lemon and cream mixture and pour into individual glasses.
4. Set in the fridge for at least 4 hours before decoration with toasted flaked almonds and mixed peel.
5. Serve with shortbread.

Shortbread

115g salted butter
55g light brown sugar
130g plain flour
40g rice flour
1 vanilla pod seeds
Demerara sugar to garnish

1. Cream the butter, vanilla seeds and sugar and add the sieved flour and rice flour.
2. Press into a tin and bake at 160^0C for about 20 minutes or light golden brown.
3. Remove from the oven and sprinkle with demerara sugar, cool and cut to size.

Swiss Roll Sponge (45cm x 20cm)

4 eggs
125g caster sugar
75g plain flour
25g cornflour

1. Sieve the flour and cornflour together.
2. Whisk the eggs together with the sugar over a water bath until light and fluffy and triple in size.
3. Whisk cold with an electric mix until thick and foamy.
4. Gently fold in the flour and cornflour.
5. Divide the mixture on greaseproof-lined baking trays and spread out the mixture evenly.
6. Bake at 210^{0}C for about 4-5 minutes or until golden brown.
7. Remove from the baking tray and cool on a cooling rack with the paper.

Swiss Roll Filling Crème Mousseline

500ml full-fat milk
40g custard powder
10g cocoa powder
200g caster sugar

1. Dilute custard powder with some of the cold milk.
2. Bring the remaining milk together with cocoa powder to the boil.
3. Add the milk to the diluted custard powder solution.
4. Return back to the heat and cook for 2 minutes.
5. Remove from the heat and stir in the sugar.
6. Place into a bowl, cover with cling film, and allow cooling.

250g butter
100g raspberry jam

1. Cream the butter until light and fluffy, then add cool but not cold custard to the butter till all combined.

Assemble

1. Spread a thin layer of jam on the sponge roulade.
2. Spread over ¾ of the custard filling.
3. Roll up, sideways and chill.
4. Decorated as required with the remaining buttercream.

Tip:

- Put ¼ of a teaspoon of cayenne pepper into the custard milk to get that chilly flavour, and use lime marmalade instead of raspberry jam.

Chocolate Fondant (4 portions)

15g sieved cacao powder
40g caster sugar

- Sieve cacao powder and add to the sugar.
- Butter moulds and dust with the above.

130g butter
130g dark chocolate
1 egg
2 egg yolk
75g caster sugar

55g self-rising flour
35g cocoa powder

1. Melt butter and chocolate over a water bath.
2. Whisk egg, yolks and sugar into a sabayon. Warm over a hot water bath until double in size; whisk cold with an electric mixer.
3. Fold in the melted chocolate /butter.
4. Fold in the sieved self-rising flour and cocoa powder.
5. Fill into the moulds and chill for at least 30 minutes.
6. Heat oven to 190^{0}C.
7. Bake for 11 minutes, depending on size.
8. Rest for 5 minutes.
9. Serve out of the mould.

Macarons

My Macaron Bible

Making macarons can be tricky, and it takes some practice. But it's a craft well learning. After all, the macaron is said to be the world's most temperamental biscuit and even professional chefs at times struggle to get it right.

French meringue

A French meringue is created by whipping together cool egg whites with caster sugar until they form a stiff consistency. The French method is the most commonly used in macaron recipes because it results in the correct texture and taste for the French macaron. The French method is the one most recommended for baking a batch of successful and authentic French macarons as they tend to be lighter and tastier with a more delicate, biscuit-like texture that melts in the mouth.

French Macarons

60g egg whites
Pinch of salt
35g caster sugar

75g ground almonds
150g icing sugar

Food colour

1. Sieve almond and icing sugar (twice).
2. Whisk egg white with a pinch of salt until triple in size.
3. Slowly add the caster sugar.
4. Once done, whisk in the food colour.
5. Add the coloured meringue to the sieved almonds.
6. Push together.
7. Pipe as required.
8. Allow to dry for 30 minutes before baking.
9. Bake at 150^0C for 12-15 minutes.

Italian Macarons

The Italian method is said to produce a more stable meringue because it uses hot sugar syrup in place of dry sugar, but the downside is that it results in macarons that are too sweet and harder to bake correctly. The Italian method is slightly more complicated than the French, as it relies on hot sugar syrup slowly whipped into egg whites to achieve its meringue. You will also need to have a sugar thermometer on hand to monitor the temperature of the sugar syrup.

Italian Meringue

Some prefer the Italian method as it is said to be more reliable than the French, but it will not produce the exact taste and texture of a French macaron. To create the Italian meringue, sugar is dissolved into water in a saucepan and brought to a boil at the soft-ball stage at 121^0C. After the syrup is created, it is slowly drizzled into the egg whites as they are whipped until the mixture forms stiff peaks and cools. Take caution while using this method, as pouring the syrup in too fast will cook the eggs and ruin the meringue.

Italian Macarons

65g ground almonds
65g icing sugar
25g raw egg whites

1. Sieve the ground almonds with icing sugar and beat together with egg white until a smooth paste has been obtained. (Add food colour optional)

Italian Meringue

65g caster sugar
20ml water
25g egg whites
Pinch of crème of tartar

1. Make an Italian meringue by boiling the caster sugar, tartar and water to 121^0C and slowly whisking into the whisk egg whites.
2. Whisk until cool and gently push into the almond paste.
3. Pipe using a plain nozzle and allow drying for about 30 minutes.
4. Heat oven to 150^0C and bake for about 10 minutes until the top is crisp
5. Cool slightly and place onto a cooling rack.

Swiss Macarons

The Swiss method is less commonly called for but may be of benefit to anyone who cannot master the technique of either the French or Italian meringue. However, it relies on whipping the meringue while it heats over a water bath, which may pose a challenge to the less experienced. The Swiss method calls for the sugar and egg whites to be whisked together as they heat over a water bath. The mixture must be constantly stirred so that the eggs do not cook. After the mixture reaches a temperature of about 50^0C, it is removed from the heat, whipped on a low setting until it cools, and then whipped on high speed until it forms stiff peaks.

Swiss Macarons

100g egg whites
70g caster sugar
100g icing sugar
50g ground almonds

1. Whisk egg white and sugar over a hot water bath to 50^0C.
2. Whisk cold on a machine.
3. Stir in food colour.
4. Push in sieved icing sugar and ground almonds.
5. Pipe using a plain nozzle and allow drying for about 30 minutes.
6. Heat oven to 150^0C and bake for about 10 minutes until the top is crisp.
7. Cool slightly and place onto a cooling rack.

Baking Macarons

Know your oven, but here are some tips:

- Bake at 150^{0}C for 8 minutes. After that, open the door to release any moisture.
- Bake for another 8 minutes.
- Don't put more than one tray in the oven, as it can create too much moisture.
- Always allow to stand before baking minutes 30minutes or until the outside is dry to the touch.

Macaron tips:

- Use egg white at room temperature, not from the fridge.
- Ensure the egg white is clean and does not contain any egg yolk.
- Ensure all equipment is squeaky clean.
- Sieve almond and icing sugar twice.
- Try not to fold ingredients but push them together to remove air.

Colouring macarons

- Use paste or powder colour, not liquids.
- Always at the end once the egg white is stiff or into the almond base mix.
- In chocolate macarons, add, in all of the recipes in this book, 25g cocoa powder.
- Always ensure colouring is fully incorporated.

Macaron Faults:

Meringue won't stiffen properly

- Dirty equipment
- Colouring added too early
- Egg white was too fresh or too cold

Macaron batter too wet or runny

- Too much flavouring or colouring (don't use liquid colours)
- Too much mixing
- Meringue was not stiff enough before adding almonds
- Incorrect measuring
- Beaten egg white was left standing too long before combing with the almonds

Macarons have pointy or lumpy shells

- Almonds not sieved enough, too many large almond pieces in batter
- Not enough mixing of the batter (if they have points once piped tap the tray on the table to flatten them out)

Macarons have greasy spots on surface

- Too much macaronnage (combined for too long)

Macarons run into each other

- Batter too runny
- Piped too close together

Macaron crack

- Batter too runny
- Batter under mixed
- Not dried long enough
- Too many trays in the oven
- Too much humidity in the oven (remember to open the oven after 8 minutes)
- Oven temperature too high

No feet at the bottom of macaron

- Batter too runny
- Not dried long enough
- Oven temperature too low

Macaron stick to baking tray or parchment paper

- Undercooked
- Not cooled enough before removing

Macarons inconsistent within one batch

- Uneven airflow in the oven (oven too full)
- Food colouring not mixed in evenly enough

Macarons hollow

- Not baked long enough
- Too many air bubbles in mixture

Macarons too soft and soggy the next day

- Shells undercooked
- Too much filling
- Filling was too wet
- Stored incorrectly (always store in airtight container in the fridge)

Ganach Macaron Fillings

Dark Chocolate	Milk Chocolate	White Chocolate
115g dark chocolate 150ml double cream	115g milk chocolate 100ml double cream	115g white chocolate 100ml double cream

Method

1. Boil cream and pour over chocolate and stir together gently.
2. When almost set, beat with a whisk in order to aerate the ganache.
3. Pipe onto the cooked macaroons.

Alcohol Ganache

60ml double cream
120g milk chocolate (or white or dark)
25ml alcohol

1. Boil cream.
2. Add the hot cream to the chocolate.
3. Stir together and add alcohol.
4. Cool until piping consistency and pipe onto the macarons.

Tip:
- Infuse the cream with coffee, herbs or orange rind.

Fruit Ganache

60g fruit puree (passionfruit, raspberry, strawberry, mango)
120g milk chocolate (or white or dark)
25ml alcohol

1. Boil fruit puree.
2. Add the hot cream to the chocolate.
3. Stir together and add alcohol.
4. Cool until piping consistency and pipe onto the macaroon.

Custard Macaron Fillings
Rosewater Custard

100g unsalted butter creamed
45ml milk
45ml double cream
1 teaspoon of rosewater
1 egg
20g sugar
10g custard powder

1. Heat milk, cream and rosewater; do not boil.
2. Whisk together egg, sugar and custard powder.
3. Pour hot rose milk over the egg mixture.
4. Return to the heat and cook out (boil until thickened).
5. Cool slightly and whisk into the beaten butter.

Lemon Custard

100g unsalted butter creamed
90ml lemon juice
Zest of 1 lemon
1 egg
20g sugar
10g custard powder

1. Heat lemon juice and zest; do not boil.
2. Whisk together egg, sugar and custard powder.
3. Pour hot lemon juice through a sieve over the egg mixture.
4. Return to the heat and cook out (boil until thickened).
5. Cool slightly and whisk into the beaten butter.

Sticky Toffee Pudding Filling

200g pitted chopped dates
20ml water
30g butter
1 tablespoon of rum
Pinch of mixed spice
1 tablespoon of dark, soft brown sugar
Drop of vanilla essence
60ml double cream

1. Heat all the above except the cream and cook for about 10 minutes.
2. When dates are soft, stir in double cream.
3. Puree and set aside to cool.
4. Once chilled slightly, beat up and pipe as required.

Welsh Cakes

225g self-rising flour
85g caster sugar
½ teaspoon of mixed spice
50g butter
50g lard
50g currents
1 egg
1 tablespoon of milk

1. Sieve flour and mixed spice, add the caster sugar and rub in the butter and lard.
2. Stir in the currents.
3. Add the beaten egg and milk and push together gently until the mix is holding together.
4. Roll on a lightly floured surface about ½ inch thick and cut into circles using a round cutter.
5. Griddle on a medium heat until golden brown.
6. Cover in caster sugar.

Parkin

1 large egg
4 tablespoons of full-fat milk
200g butter
200g golden syrup
85g black treacle
85g light soft brown sugar
100g medium oatmeal (ground-up oats not too fine)
250g self-rising flour
1 teaspoon of ground ginger
1 teaspoon of ground cinnamon

1. Heat the oven to 160^{0}C. Grease a deep 9-inch square cake tin and line with baking parchment.
2. Beat the egg and milk together with a fork.
3. Gently melt the syrup, treacle, sugar and butter together in a large pan until the sugar has dissolved. Remove from the heat.
4. Mix together the oatmeal, flour, cinnamon and ginger and stir into the syrup mixture, followed by the egg and milk.
5. Pour the mixture into the tin and bake for 50 minutes - 1 hour until the cake feels firm and a little crusty on top. Cool in the tin, then wrap in more parchment and foil and keep for 3-5 days before eating it. It will become softer and stickier the longer you leave it. Keep for up to 2 weeks.

Battenberg

Almond Cake

225g butter
225g caster sugar
225g self-rising flour
85g ground almonds
3 eggs
1 teaspoon of vanilla essence
½ teaspoon of almond essence
1 tablespoon of milk

1. Cream the butter, sugar, vanilla and almond essence until light and fluffy.
2. Slowly add the eggs.
3. Fold in the flour, ground almonds and milk.
4. Bake in an 8-inch cake tin at 175^{0}C for about 25 minutes or until springy to the touch.

Rose Cake

225g butter
225g caster sugar
225g self-rising flour
85g ground almonds
3 eggs
1 teaspoon of vanilla essence
1 tablespoon of rosewater
1 tablespoon of milk
Pink food colouring

1. Cream the butter, sugar, vanilla, rosewater and pink colouring until light and fluffy.
2. Slowly add the eggs.
3. Fold in the flour, ground almonds and milk.
4. Bake in an 8-inch cake tin at 175^0C for about 25 minutes or springy to the touch.

Assemble
1. Cut the skin of both baked and cooled cakes.
2. Cut each cake into two slices.
3. Cut the crust of each cake slice.
4. Cut out two circles of each cake slice, and you end up with three crustless cake circles. Swap the cake rings of the almond sponges with the rose sponges and fit the cut pieces back together.

200g apricot jam
1 tablespoon of rosewater
500g white marzipan

1. Heat the apricot jam, then sieve and stir in the rose water.
2. Brush some over the top of one of the sponges and top with an alternating sponge. Repeat to stack up all the layers.
3. Brush some more jam all over the top and sides of the cake and cover in marzipan.

Chapter 8

Pop-up, teas and the Jamaican story garden

Recipes

1. Jamaican Story Garden Hummingbird Cake

2. Jamaican Bun and Cheese

3. Lemon Drizzle cake

4. Opera Cake

5. Tea Cakes

6. Cocoa Tea

7. Ginger Beer

8. Sorrel Syrup

Jamaican Story Garden Hummingbird Cake

White Chocolate Lime Cake

320ml coconut milk
100g white chocolate
Zest of 2 limes
170g butter
360g caster sugar
4 eggs
25ml vanilla essence
285g plain flour
3g baking soda
14g baking powder
50g desiccated coconut

1. Grease and line a 10-inch baking tin.
2. Heat the coconut milk and, melt the chocolate in the milk, chill the chocolate milk.
3. Cream the butter, lime zest and sugar until light and fluffy.
4. Combine the eggs with the vanilla essence.
5. Add the eggs to the base mix, one at a time.
6. Sieve the flour, baking powder and baking soda and mix with the coconut.
7. Fold in half the chocolate milk into the base mix, followed by half the flour mixture repeat until all is combined.
8. Pour into the prepared tin and bake at 175^{0}C for about 45 minutes.
9. Check by inserting a skewer into the centre of the cake. If it comes out clean, the cake is ready to take out. Remove from the tin and cool on a cooling rack.

White Chocolate Mango Filling

40g mango puree
40g caster sugar
40g glucose
2 leaves of gelatine
225g melted white chocolate
300ml semi whipped cream

200g mango puree

1. Soak the gelatine in cold water.
2. Boil 40g of the mango puree, sugar and glucose.
3. Remove from the heat, add gelatine.
4. Add melted chocolate and let cool.
5. Just before setting, fold in the cream.

Passionfruit Syrup

100g passionfruit juice
25g caster sugar

1. Boil passionfruit juice and sugar.

Assemble

1. Cut the cold chocolate cake into three.
2. Place the top layer upside down back into the cake tin, which is lined with baking paper.
3. Soak the cake in a third of passion fruit syrup.
4. Spread half the filling onto the cake and drizzle mango puree onto the filling using a fork to marble in cover with the middle layer of the cake.
5. Soak with another third of the passion fruit syrup.
6. Spread the remaining filling onto the middle layer and drizzle mango puree onto the filling using a fork to marble in; cover with the bottom layer upside down.
7. Soak the top layer with the remaining third of the passion fruit syrup.
8. Set in the fridge for 2 hours.
9. Once chilled down, turn upside down out of the tin.

Fruit Compote

1 small pineapple diced
1 lime juice
1 mango diced
2 tablespoons of chopped mint

1. Combine and serve with the cake.

Jamaican Bun (500g loaf tin or an 8-inch cake tin)

450g self-rising flour
1 teaspoon of baking powder
2 teaspoons of ground cinnamon
½ teaspoon of ground pimento
2 teaspoons of grated nutmeg
1 teaspoon of ground ginger
½ teaspoon of salt

80g butter
Zest of 1 lime
90g dark soft brown sugar
1 tablespoon of vanilla essence
60g molasses
1 egg
250ml dark beer
150g sultanas

1. Sieve flour, baking powder, spices and salt.
2. Melt butter, sugar, molasses, vanilla and lime zest, cool down.
3. Stir the egg into the beer.
4. Fold in the sugar syrup and beer mixture into the flour mix.
5. Lastly, fold in the sultanas
6. Bake at 180^0C for about 45-50 minutes or springy to the touch.
7. Serve with mature cheddar cheese.

Lemon Drizzle Cake (8-inch round cake tin)

225g unsalted butter
225g caster sugar
Zest of 2 lemons
4 eggs
200g self-rising flour
50g ground almonds
½ teaspoon of ground ginger

Juice of 2 Lemons
50g granulate sugar

1. Cream the soft butter, sugar and lemon zest until light and fluffy.
2. Gradually add the beaten eggs.
3. Fold in the sieved flour, ground almonds and ginger.
4. Bake at 160^0C for about 30-40 minutes or until golden brown and springy to the touch.
5. Combine the lemon juice with the granulated sugar and drizzle over the baked cake whist still warm.

Tip:
- I serve mine with thick Greek yoghurt.

Opera Cake

Jaconde Sponge

40g plain sieved flour
100g ground almonds
30g melted butter
4 eggs
150g caster sugar

1. Sieve flour and ground almonds and set aside.
2. Melt butter and set aside.
3. Whisk eggs and sugar over a water bath until doubled in size. Whisk cold, using an electric mixer, into a thick foam.

6 egg whites
Pinch of salt
20g caster sugar

1. Whisk to a French meringue by whisking the egg whites with a pinch of salt until tripled in size, and slowly whisk in the sugar.
2. Fold the meringue into the egg foam, followed by the dry ingredients.
3. Lastly, fold in the melted butter.
4. Spread onto three trays (20cm by 30cm).
5. Bake at 210^0C for 4-5 minutes.
6. Cut the baked almond sponge in 3 equal pieces.

Italian Buttercream

90g egg whites
150g caster sugar
50ml water
1 teaspoon of glucose
340g unsalted butter
2 teaspoons of coffee essence (50g hot water with 2 teaspoons of instant coffee)

1. Whisk the egg white to a soft peak.
2. Boil water, sugar and glucose to 121^0C.
3. Add the hot sugar syrup to the whisked egg white by continuously whisking.
4. Keep whisking until cooled, 5- 8 minutes.
5. Gradually add the unsalted butter while continuing to whisk until a smooth cream is obtained.
6. Flavour with coffee essence for the opera filling.

Rum Coffee Syrup

100ml water
60g sugar
1 teaspoon of instant coffee
20ml rum

1. Boil water, sugar and coffee, and add the rum.

Opera Cake Assembly

Chocolate Ganache
Rum Syrup
Jaconde Sponge
Coffee Butter Cream
Rum Syrup
Jaconde Sponge
Coffee Butter Cream
Rum Syrup
Jaconde Sponge

Chocolate Ganache

100ml double cream
1 teaspoon of glucose
100g dark chocolate

1. Boil cream and glucose.
2. Pour over the chocolate and gently stir together.
3. Glaze the top of the opera, allow to chill for 2 hours and cut as required.

Vegan Tea Cakes (17 pieces)

900g strong flour
Good pinch of salt
60g sheer butter
60g dark soft brown sugar
30g fresh yeast (or 15g dried yeast)
570g soya milk
120g sultanas
120g mixed peel
2 teaspoons of ground cinnamon
2 teaspoons of vanilla essence

1. Gently warm milk and vanilla set aside.
2. Sieve flour and salt and combine with the cinnamon.
3. Dissolve the yeast in the warm milk and add 4 tablespoons of the sieved flour. Allow to froth for about 20 minutes.
4. Once bubbled up, add the remaining ingredients and knead until smooth.
5. Rest until double in size.
6. Scale into 125g pieces and roll into rolls. Lightly flatten the tea cake before brushing with soya milk.
7. Prove until double in size and bake at 180^{0}C until golden brown.

Cocoa Tea

300ml water
1000ml coconut milk
30g 100% chocolate (if you can't find 100%, use a 90% one)
1 cinnamon stick
½ teaspoon of grated nutmeg
4 torn up bay leaves
50g light brown sugar (or more to taste)

1. Boil water, cinnamon stick, nutmeg, and bay leaves. Reduce the heat and simmer for 15 minutes.
2. Take off the heat and infuse for at least 30 minutes. The longer, the better.
3. Strain the flavored water and heat up gently with the chocolate.
4. Once melted, add the coconut milk and sugar, and warm up; do not boil.

The Jamaican Story Garden Ginger Beer Welcome Drink

250g grated peeled ginger
200ml water
100g light brown sugar
100ml lime juice
Sparkling water.

1. Boil water, remove from the heat and add grated ginger.
2. Let stand for at least 24 hours.
3. Strain off the ginger from the water.
4. Make a dry caramel with half of the sugar, adding the ginger water.
5. Add the remaining sugar and simmer for 10 minutes.
6. Cool and add 100ml of fresh lime juice.
7. Top with a sparkling water ratio of 1:1.

The Jamaican Story Garden Sorrel Syrup Welcome Drink

500ml water
50g dried sorrel (hibiscus flowers)
8 pieces of cloves
1 cinnamon stick
¼ teaspoon of nutmeg
1 tablespoon of grated peeled ginger
200g light brown sugar

1. Sterilise a bottle or jar with hot water.
2. Place water, sorrel and all spices into a pan and bring to a boil.
3. Simmer for 5 minutes and leave for about an hour or overnight.
4. Strain the spiced water, add the sugar and once dissolved, pour into the sterilised jars.
5. Serve with sparking water, lots of ice and a slice of lime.

Tip:
• Add a shot of rum for that extra punch